THE FOUNDATIONS OF MANAGEMENT

WHAT YOU
SHOULD KNOW
ABOUT

THE
FOUNDATIONS
OF
MANAGEMENT

By ROY A. LINDBERG

1973 OCEANA PUBLICATIONS, INC.

DOBBS FERRY, NEW YORK

Number 21 in the
BUSINESS ALMANAC SERIES

3 84457

Each volume in the Business Almanac Series is designed
to introduce you to an aspect of modern American Business
theory and practice.

© Copyright 1973 by Oceana Publications, Inc.

Library of Congress Cataloging in Publication Data

Lindberg, Roy A
  What you should know about the foundations of
management.

  (Business almanac series, no. 21)
  1. Industrial management. I. Title. II. Title:
The foundations of management.
HD31.L474   658.4   73-3319
ISBN 0-379-11221-3

HD
31
. L474
1973

Manufactured in the United States of America

Our rate of progress is such that an individual human being, of ordinary length of life, will be called upon to face novel situations which find no parallel in his past. The fixed person, for the fixed duties, who in other societies was such a godsend, in the future will be a public danger.

--Alfred North Whitehead

TABLE OF CONTENTS

I.
INTRODUCTION

This is a small book. What it has to say does not require many words. Things that are true never do; things that are false seldom survive terseness.

The theme of the book and the thesis for which it seeks support is that management, to be performed competently, requires more than experience or knowledge, that it also requires perceptions that may never be proven by any form of interaction with the outside world. These perceptions form the basis of management as each manager practices it. Thus the book is about the foundations of management rather than the principles of the discipline itself.

The idea for the book arose the day the author, who had long despaired of his lack of assurance in dealing with business matters, came to realize that he would never be experienced enough or have enough facts at hand to make consistently dependable business decisions or even a respectable decision each time one was required of him. He came to realize that, as it is true of men generally, no businessman can have nearly enough externally derived knowledge (through experience, study, or research) usually to decide well.

The reasons for that are both existential and logical. As to the first, no manager can live long enough to have prior experience of or acquire enough knowledge (however garnered) of every situation he will be faced with. One cannot, for example, have applicable experience of the novel or the unique. It is impossible to experience an event yet to happen or to have directly usable experience of an event that will not arise again. The loss of virginity, for example, precludes the possibility of having to deal with the loss again.

As to the second, while the body of current business knowledge is swollen with much pertinent material, it is far from reconciling its many conflicting views. The discipline, therefore, is in many respects too cumbersome and un-utilitarian. By the time one has fought his way through the bulk of it to the truths it contains, the situation to be resolved has usually expired for want of decision.

These are among the reasons why managers must have something more than direct or surrogate experience to perform well. A sound basis for action can be built neither from a manager's own experiences nor through study of the experience of others.

That managing achieves its purpose in part through the exercise of what is learned from contact with the external environment cannot, of course, be denied. But, it is evident that the successes of management emanate from considerably more than that. Every manager needs to know something about specific matters, i.e. return on investment, discounted cash flow, linear programming, order point/order quantity determination, the fundamentals of marketing, production, finance, and so forth. But such knowledge will never be scaled large enough to bridge gaps in experience or be sufficiently adaptable to enable its possessor to avoid disaster in dealing with every situation that will confront him. Good managerial decisions will always require (direct or indirect) inputs from reason and imagination as well as from experience. Such inputs, however, cannot arise out of particular knowledge alone. General knowledge - knowledge that transcends the limitations of experience and research - is also needed.

Though a manager cannot through experience and acquired knowledge alone be prepared to deal effectively with every kind of decision required of him, he need not despair or put off deciding. He must make decisions whether he possesses relevant experience or not. This being the case, the question then arises, on what basis can he ever be justified in being confident in his decision powers?

The answer lies in the possession of managerially relevant generalizations so simple, cogent, and persuasive they must be labeled beliefs, values, convictions. To be able to decide well in novel situations or in situations that do not allow time to gather and analyze all the information available, the manager must have guides to action in which he has complete confidence. Without such guides no amount of experience or information will enable him generally to reach sound conclusions.

Though no manager can possibly gain sufficient experience to become through that avenue alone the "generalist" so much talked about. Generalists are both possible and needed in business. A true generalist, then, is a manager who, despite his shortcomings of specific, applicable experience and knowledge,

2

has decision guides in the form of concepts large, accommodating, earthy, and attractive enough to be capable in all situations of keeping him from making serious errors.

Much less than managing well, even to benefit from experience requires that managers have such concepts. The variety of experiences emerging from managing to be comprehensible requires not only specific knowledge of details or facets but knowledge capable of operating on particulars and relating them meaningfully. The hue and cry to "get down to the nitty-gritty," when made in the absence of something to get down from, sponsors a fruitless pursuit. In management, reliance on information in the form of facts or data is misplaced when it exists outside the embrace of fundamentals capable of organizing the information. The fundamentals must be hypotheses of sufficient scale to be able to give meaning (identify, classify, give weight to) the full range of phenomena emerging from or related to the purposes, operations, and management of profit-making enterprise.

The problem with such hypotheses is that they describe the realities they aim at only in the most general terms, and general terms fail to interest most people. But, if he is to be effective, a manager must be familiar with and understand such definitions as they apply to the field of business. If he comes from a specialized background, such as accounting, where the rules and reference points are relatively fixed, he must learn to be comfortable in a field where the guidelines and milestones are less obvious and more complex than those of his specialty. Finding one's way safely in management requires the vision, the scale of understanding that can be given and supported only by the broadest and most deeply held concepts.

The holding of such concepts is not in itself, of course, sufficient to ensure rational managerial behavior. The concepts must also be mutually compatible and woven into a comprehensive view. Therefore, it can be said that every successful manager has a philosophy - that is, a body of basic and integrated views, tenets, or convictions. Without sound convictions woven together in some form of conceptual unity the possession of all the facts in the world will not enable a manager to arrive quickly at sound and defensible conclusions. Conversely, the manager's use of specifics cannot be generally productive until a matrix, a ground system that gives meaning and place to every business fact or event has been created.

The need for an integrated view does not imply there can be or should be one common to all holders. Contrary to the notions of many who are working to develop a universal and transferable management discipline, the concepts, principles, fundamentals entering into each manager's view need not (and, in fact, cannot) be the same, nor can they remain the same throughout the working lifetime of each manager. They vary from manager to manager, and from one period to another in the life of each manager.

For generations men interested in business enterprises, have been looking for a single concept - a raison d'etre - that explains a business enterprise and provides understanding of how to act in any business situation. None has yet been found; nor is there a sign that one may be found. But some ideas exist that, fused together, can be used in the place of a singular rubric.

In the following sections a number of propositions are stated that appear to the author to describe the basic character of business and management and managing as they exist in a "free" economy. The propositions are offered with full recognition of their logical or empirical vulnerability, but with the confidence that they represent a step in the right direction.

In the opinion of the author, no manager can afford to be without the support of something akin to them. To operate without hypotheses broad enough to give him a basis for understanding the phenomena he is confronted by and deciding questions he has no experience or knowledge to cover is to walk blindly toward the future. The greater the responsibility of the manager, the greater is his need to hold propositions similar to those suggested.

The book does not represent an effort to distill the entire body of management knowledge down to the smallest number of constituent propositions; only those sufficiently removed from factual demonstration are of concern here. Oddly enough, these are the ones that are needed most. This raises the interesting possibility that the most important propositions for the manager are those furthest removed from provability.). Familiar matters, such as return on investment, discounted cash flow, and the ABC principle in inventory management can be expressed in propositinal form, but they are easily demonstrated and ill-suited as integrating hypotheses. The propositions in these pages stop well short of being technological descriptions. They are in the nature

4

of things we normally call hypotheses, concepts, convictions.

The majority of propositions that follow are generally familiar, a few even awfully so. Some will not strike the reader as having any importance and a few are likely to be rejected as being totally unacceptable. No harm. Consideration of the propositions offered in these pages cannot lead to worse than their rejection because they seem obvious, unrealistic or, even, absurd. On the other hand, consideration of them may stimulate new perspectives or ideas of value to the manager.*

The propositions stated are thought to be important as much because of the deductions that can be drawn from them as for what they say directly. The criterion of their worth need be no more than that they are important to someone. They are offered here in that spirit and as examples of their kind.

In the opinion of the author there is a managerial imperative that says each manager is obligated to provide himself with a basis for action in which he has confidence. To fail in trying to do what must be done is forgivable and, sometimes, even admirable, but to have failed to have tried at all because the means has not been provided for knowing what must be done and how to do it - subjective as that knowledge may be - is slothful and unforgivable. Since choices can and must be made, the manager who does not provide himself with such means is committing a managerial "sin."

---

* Shortly after this book was written an article came to the author's attention that in a number of respects offers support or counterpoint to many of the propositions offered in the following pages. It is well worth reading and is the first of the items composing the appendix.

II.
ON THE NATURE OF BUSINESS

Few questions have been more pawed over in recent years than the question of what a business enterprise is. There are, of course, any number of answers, depending upon the perspective of the inquirer and the objectives of the inquiry. A business can be defined in many ways, among them in legal, sociological, or entrepreneurial terms. However, all businesses have common characteristics, the most important of which can be stated in something like the following propositions:

A business' prime responsibility is to survive.

A business does not survive gratuitously.

A business survives by filling needs.

A business is profit-contingent.

A business is complex.

A business is dynamic.

A business is a tension system.

A business forms a system.

A business has inertia.

A business must innovate.

A business requires decision-making.

A business is information-dependent.

A business is a social organization.

A business deserves employee loyalty.

Let us examine each of these characteristics more fully.

A Business' Prime Responsibility Is To Survive

Every business enterprise must make the aim to survive first among its objectives. When other objectives come before survival, death cannot be far off.

If this proposition is true, profit maximization should never be the principal goal of business nor should immediate profit ever be first among intentions. Profit is a resultant of being successfully in business. Sound business decisions do not always produce current profit but they always contribute to the firm's perpetuation. Profits can often be maximized in the short run, but this is usually done at the expense of survivability.

The proposition holds important implications for the work of the manager. It implies, among other things, that managers should direct their energies more to long-term results than immediate ones, more to tomorrow than to today, more to opportunities than problems. It implies that managers should work to keep the enterprise lean than most profitable. Where the greatest care taken on a current basis is to fulfill the needs of a business, the best profit in the long run is likely to result.

A Business Does Not Survive Gratuitously

Survival in business cannot be incidental or accidental. Over the years it can only be a result of deliberate, intelligent, and well-executed effort. One of the essential tasks of each manager, therefore is to become and remain aware of the elements upon which his company's survival depends. Once they have been identified his effort should be directed toward the provision of those elements or protection of those already in existence.

Identification of survival elements frequently turns up strange dependencies - some good, some bad. For example, survival in one speciality manufacturing company was tied to a 65-year-old engineer who single-handedly dealt with customer problems, developed new markets from his customer contacts, and provided liaison between sales and the factory. In a particular wholesale business it was the renewable distribution contract with a nationally-known consumer product that opened the door for all the other products the company sold. Determination of whether these dependencies are good or bad depends upon the risks involved and the perspectives chosen. Whether good or bad, the dependencies exist, and must be dealt with according to their importance to the future life of their firms.

A Business Survives By Filling Needs

All businesses survive by filling needs external to their own. No business has ever come into being or is sustained by being its only customer or providing goods or services that are not needed. The needs served may not be crucial to human life (not many Rolls Royces are built yearly) and they may not always be universal (not everyone likes pumpernickel) but the needs are, nonetheless, real for all that.

The implications of this view are profound. They make such seemingly vital questions of the day, as the question of business ownership, unimportant. The view implies, among other things, that a business "belongs" more to the markets and customers it serves than to its owners and employees. In turn, it implies that a business "belongs" more to its employees than to its owners. Further, it obviates the idea so often held by entrepreneurs that "I" built the business, or that "I" created the market for this product. No business, however small, or market has ever been built solely by one person.

It is impossible to build a commercial enterprise where there is no need for its products or services. Therefore, the entrepreneur can as realistically be looked upon as an exploiter of opportunity as he can be looked upon as a builder. Those who think otherwise do so in ignorance of the realities involved and are prone to making serious errors in business judgment.

The practical point of all this is that a business cannot fail to keep a watchful eye on the market(s) it serves and institutes unfailingly, every improvement possible in servicing them. The necessity to improve the enterprise has a larger scope than the rights of ownership or current profitability, and serving one of the latter before serving the market is fraught with danger. For example, when the privileges of business ownership come first, the possibilities that management will take its eye off its market(s) and respond to lesser needs - such as diverting business funds to personal uses or to pet projects - become almost certainties. And, a business that stresses current profit at the expenses of future profitability is more likely to find itself on the ropes than firms in which long-term profit is deemed most important.

A Business Is Profit-Contingent

The proposition that the life of an enterprise is contingent on profit may seem beneath consideration, having received so much attention through the years. But it is fascination to observe how completely, in being agreed to, it seems to have been ignored. The proposition must be kept in view, nonetheless, because profit has as much value as a measure of business health as it has in and by itself.

There is no need to apologize for profit. The concept of profit is not simply economic - it is characteristic of life generally. Every living thing is a profit system, the human body being no exception. Each body utilizes less than it ingests and stores the excess as glycogen in the liver. When intake balances consumption in the long run the body becomes comatose. When consumption exceeds intake for long death ensues.

A business works the same way; in the end it must have something left over after it sells what it buys and produces. In economic terms, the survival of business ultimately depends upon its providing goods and services at better prices than its competitors or better goods and services at competitive prices.

Management is very much the discipline of economic production, the art of making the most of resources in the production of goods and services at best cost. Profit, therefore, is the truest of all marks of corporate health.

A Business Is Complex

A business must compete if it is to survive, and to compete it must constantly change. The environment in which it operates - social, scientific, physical, cybernetic - is constantly changing and each firm is acted upon by all these interacting relationships. Hence a business is an incredibly complex institution.

The demands on business are rising steadily and steeply as attested to by the rise in:

10

1. the number of factors dealt with (government regulations, changing distribution practices, etc.)
2. logistical volumes and quantities (production runs, sales, etc.)
3. communication volumes and speeds
4. executive turnover and mobility

These and many similar changes have made businesses among the most complex of human institutions.

It may at first appear too obvious and, therefore, unimportant to keep in mind that a business is complex. It is common, however, to find business problems being treated simplistically. For example, a manager will state that if only he had a good plant manager, or if only competition really knew its own costs, or if only those cheap imports could be controlled, or if only that union wasn't so thick-headed, or if he only had a computer -- then his problem in running the business would be over. Such views are deceptive. Business is so complex that one-shot answers are rarely effective.

A Business Is Dynamic

A fruitful way to look at a business is to view it as an energy field. Forces in every company that is more than a corporate shell are always in flux, and it is the unique task of management to see that these forces produce useful results. Taking another tack, forces in being (one definition of a company) cannot be productive of intended results unless the fact of their existence is recognized and they are directed by that special set of forces subsumed under the name of management.

To understand that a business is dynamic one only has to see that a business, like a ship, may be in equilibrium but only as the result of constant and interacting forces (every ship is in the process of sinking and can be kept afloat only through equilibrium maintaining efforts). Similarly, every business is subject to forces (influences or activities) that will overwhelm it if left unattended for long. No captain can concern himself exclusively with piloting and navigating. He must also see to it that rust is chipped and painting done, the well is sounded, bilges are pumped, and that plates are tested for strength. In the same fashion, no businessman can safely concern himself with thinking about and planning the future course of the business without also seeing to the control of costs, employee productivity, and reduction of waste.

Formal organization offers a clear example of corporate dynamism. Every structure tends from the first of its existence to disorganize just as the universe at all times tends toward entrophy (the state in which boundaries and identities disappear). Structural differentiation can be maintained only through special effort. The same is true of all other aspects of business; unless work is expended to maintain them as designed they will change, usually unfavorably.

A Business Is A Tension System

In any entity in which there are many factors at work there is bound to be conflict or counter-productive behavior. A business enterprise is an arena of many active factors.

Men have long thought that a sound business is indicated by the relative absence of contention, conflict, "noise." Management has traditionally been regarded as "oil" to the gears of business machinery; that where management is effective the only noise that will be heard is that of coins entering the till.

Little could be further from the truth. A sensitive, vigorous, alert business is characterized by the sounds of argument, of contests between views and opinions stemming from differing experiences of and responses to the many factors at work, every one of which runs in some way counter to some other factor.

Look at it this way: an enterprise is a collection of activities that accomplishes the enterprise's objectives by acting in opposition in the same fashion that a muscle accomplishes work by contracting between two points of attachment. The functions of a business accomplish their work in the same fashion. For example, a firm prospers by stimulating individual thinking but also ensuring coordination of individual effort. A further illustration lies in the opposition between formal organization and counter-organization behavior. The benefits of formal organization would quickly be offset by the losses caused by increased rigidity if it were not that human ingenuity soon after the establishment of a given organizational design finds its way around the less important constraints. In short, a business gets things done through things working against each other as much as it does

12

through things working together.

A Business Forms A System

No single proposition has more worth as a guide to managerial cognition and action than the idea that each business forms a system, a union of interdependent parts responding as a whole to its environment. The possession of this idea, alone, gives managers a respectable basis for taking action in situations foreign to them. The idea can be used to detect problems ordinarily overlooked, such as imbalances between activities that in themselves are well-designed and established, or serve as the basis for decision-making in situations not covered by experience. In a system known as a business one excellence denotes other excellences; one deficiency denotes other deficiencies. That quality offers managers a natural blueprint for analysis, troubleshooting, and adjustment.

The statement that each business forms a system should not be taken to mean that, because it is a system, it has many qualities in common with other systems (businesses) - favorable or not. Systems have individual "personalities" and behavioral differences corresponding to those among human beings. Different as they are, however, they are all "wholes." There are no deranged companies, in the sense that there are companies whose behavioral patterns are truly contradictions. Even dying companies form systems - universes of elements that, though they may not be survival-oriented are nonetheless integrated.

It is this fact that makes investigating along system lines so profitable. A company going down the drain cannot fail to manifest its shortcomings dramatically in the form of compensations for deficiencies. Examples are the high volumes of decision-making that accompany the failure to provide viable policies, the retention of executive deadwood that parallels the failure to know what is happening to the business, the vast amount of communicating that takes place in the absence of understanding. If the deficiencies are not always visible, the compensations are. A serious inquirer can always be sure that he can catch the ends of string that he can follow through the tangled skein of corporate affairs.

It should be remembered that all human systems have individual characters because this quality prevents business performance standards being applied simplistically. Firms become aware of themselves as systems and develop personalities that determine how they cope with problems: who they will admit to membership, how they defend themselves against threats, how they communicate, organize, and build goals, and so forth. Recognition of these traits without sentimentality or moral judgment is as important to arriving at a fair understanding of how a given firm is doing as an intensive knowledge of business economics.

A Business Has Inertia

Because it operates as a system a business cannot be easily changed or redirected. Introduced changes are always parochial; they can only affect parts of the enterprise, never the total. They usually have far less than hoped-for influence on the overall performance or direction of the total enterprise. It is not far fetched to say that every effort made to change the system in some way is met with a counter-effort, an effort to keep things as they are. An enterprise is a wonderfully adaptive system, and useful change - that is, permanent and productive change - can be brought about only through painstaking, intelligent and, oftentimes, prolonged effort.

One of the common mistakes made by managers is to assume that, because the business environment is constantly changing, each enterprise tends to change at the same rate. But this assumption is blind to the fact that a business enterprise has considerable weight and directional movement and is not lightly moved out of its habitual course. A fair portion of the energy of the typical firm is spent on a continuing basis to maintain internal stability rather than stability of external relationships (with the market, with competitor behavior, et al). The first kind of stability entails no change, the second entails change. To maintain stable external relationships usually requires change.

In short, beneficial change is sometimes brought about only through altering familiar and desired relationships. It should never be assumed, therefore, that any change is welcome or has a good chance of survival without a significant investment of effort and power.

A Business Must Innovate

The proposition that a business must innovate is reflected poorly in general business practice. If this statement has any support it surely must be in the high turnover among the largest 100 companies during this century. Most of the companies who disappeared from the class failed to bring in and implement new ideas. The death of some of these companies can be directly linked to their adherence to familiar paths as a way of business life. (American Locomotive and Baldwin-Lima-Hamilton pinned their salvation on bigger and better steam locomotives 20 years after the concepts of diesel electric power were proven viable, and when they did switch to diesels they inadvisedly applied much of the manufacturing technology of steam engines to diesel power.)

Innovation should be consciously practiced in the guts of a company as well as at the top. The lack of systematic efforts to renew the purposes, objectives or technology in an enterprise is a sure sign of vulnerability to smashing blows from competitors. The time has arrived when each business must bring its innovative efforts to something comparable to the levels of scientific advancement.

It has been stated that a business must compete, which means it must consistently change. The environment in which it operates - social, scientific, physical, cybernetic - is constantly changing and in the process constantly creates new dangers and opportunities. Hence, it might almost be sensible to say that a major task of management is the introduction of change for the sake of change (the sake being the seizing of those advantages created only by change).

A Business Requires Decision-Making

Every business is dependent upon decision-making because no business can operate successfully on the basis of once-determined courses of action. Daily situations arise calling for fresh decisions.

To be well run, a business depends on reasoned choices as well as on initiative and attention to detail. Originality, brilliant intuitions, and hard work cannot by themselves assure the survival of a firm. Also needed are intelligent choices made between the alternatives imposed by the real world. Poor choices or choices not made easily outweigh fresh ideas, good luck, and material wealth.

The character, rate and "thrust" of decision-making are prime pieces of evidence in measuring and looking for ways to increase the effectiveness of a business. Highly repetitive decision-making, for example, even when done well, does not always betoken administrative efficiency. Areas of highly repetitive events should always be considered for coverage by clearly-stated policies. To take another example, high volume decision-making by a key executive in the place of lower level decision-making can only hurt the business economically.

A Business Is Information Dependent

Because it must make decisions it follows that the quality of a firm's performance relates to the quality of information it uses and the quality of its information usage. All going businesses depend upon information for successful passage to the future. In businesses going down the place of information is taken by things that do not permit objective or flexible use - such as prejudices and opinions.

Effective managers are heavy users of information. Though they are, as this book claims, deeply committed people, they are nonetheless, information-oriented. To effectively identify necessities and choices takes a good deal of information. However, the view that managers are users of information, and the better they use information the more effective they are likely to be, is another example of a proposition honored more in word than in action. Most managers still rely more on "getting along" and "getting by" than on being well informed and choosing well.

The idea that a business is dependent on information stems from the fact that businesses and their environments and constantly changing. To maintain equilibrium (stay in business) the enter prise must expend effort to counter the unstabilizing forces. Designing and exercising these efforts effectively takes information --information that is adequate, relevant, and affordable.

There is another difference. The volume of decision making in a poorly run company may not be less than in a good one. But there is a distinct difference in the kinds of decisions made be-

16

tween the two companies. In the well-managed company decisions relate to new events and the future. In the poorly managed company they relate to repeated events and only to today. Few signs are more clearly indicative of ill health in business than decision-making focusing on the same decisions. Since, however, to most managers the power to decide is comforting and adherence to policies thought to be restrictive, many companies exhibit the redundant decision syndrome.

One of the things companies do most poorly is provide information with these qualities. The reasons for that probably relate to the imperfect education for business of most executives and personalistic interpretations of the roles of leadership, individual contribution, and business judgment.

The point has been made that the task of managing is much more complicated than that of the scientist - the chemist, the physicist, the biologist. That managers must deal with more factors and relationships than the scientist is obvious. What is not so obvious is that if managers and their firms are to meet competition and survive there will have to be more and better knowledge of causal relationships between business variables than is now generally possessed. This fact leads, inevitably, to the conclusion that managers in the future are going to have to make decisions more than they have to date on the basis of empirically derived information.

That means managers are going to have to give up their reliance on the fabric they sit on. The executive who manages by the seat of his pants is the source of most business disasters today.

A Business Is A Social Organization

That a business is a social organization may seem to be a "motherhood" statement, but the truth of it is reflected in managerial action far less than its validity justifies. Until a firm is dealt with as a social structure it cannot be made to perform adequately as an economic entity.

Many firms are still dealt with purely as production institutions, within which the conditions of work are determined by the machines and processes employed. In such firms the wealth of relevant information from behavioral research has yet to make impact.

Yet, it is not the size or usefulness of its computer, the effectiveness of its cost system, its line of credit, nor the charisma of its chief executive which determine the success of a company nearly so much as its ability to employ people to their satisfaction. If a company has nothing going for it except people satisfied in their work it will probably survive. If it has everything going for it except that, sooner or later it will have to "flop."

Creating the climate in which individuals can work cooperatively yet find opportunity for individual growth and contribution is a taxing, never-ending process. Because it is the most sophisticated and variegated resource of all, manpower does not provide the ease of administration of resources the usage of which can be easily measured, such as money and materials.

However, recent developments have provided hope that it may be possible to objectively measure states of personal involvement and the contributions of supportive atmospheres to productivity and profitability. Human resources accounting is one such development; and even if it turns out that it cannot conveniently yield the measurability needed, it may, at least, teach managers to treat their people as assets instead of costs.

One thing is clear: if we are to succeed in using human resources better we will have to learn to build new and better kinds of organizations. Some think we are learning now. Jay W. Forrester, of M.I.T., sees emerging soon a recognizable trend toward organizational forms that will provide individual satisfactions more than constraints. Computers, he predicts, will serve to increase human satisfactions and effectiveness in business work.

The need for new formats may have more fundamental basis than improved employee utilization. Many informed persons see the emergence of new kinds of corporate organizations as an absolute requisite if society as we know it is to survive.

A Business Deserves Employee Loyalty

There is no current alternative to business enterprise. If enterprise breaks down our society will be deeply threatened. We cannot forage now - life can no longer survive without the institutions that clothe and feed it. Society has, in the logistical sense, passed the point of no return.

There is a moral imperative buried in the view that firms are now societal necessities; namely, that the industrial enterprise is deserving of and entitled to demand the best contribution from all its members. Not because of the compensation paid employees for their services, but because damaging the enterprise, impeding productivity, raises the costs of fulfilling everyone's needs. Needs fulfilled at higher costs damages living standards, national economic health, and personal freedom. Accordingly, each employee, whatever role he plays in his firm's affairs has a responsibility to strengthen his firm and maintain it regardless of the circumstances of his employment, quality of his supervision, or his attitudes toward work. Otherwise he and his, as well as society at large will suffer.

That responsibility cannot be displaced by any other. There can be no personal need or group identification so great that it should be put ahead of a firm's welfare. For example, the need for greater income or goals of a professional or craft union should not be served at the price of damaging the firm's survivability (nor should a firm be forced to survive to meet legislated or humane standards of employment). The corollary of that, of course, is that judgments of what is damaging or not should be made impartially. But that is another story, the telling of which would require a book unto itself.

III.
ON THE NATURE OF MANAGEMENT

The reasons why businesses decline and die are many. But the common reasons are few and splinters from the same block: the failure to apply available management knowledge.

Far less than half of new enterprises survive their first five years. The majority of the failures are caused by managerial incompetence.

Growing awareness of the devasting effects of poor management, coupled with increasing company size, decline in ownership control, and growing business competition, is stimulating interest in management. Men are learning that management often looks better than it performs, and that much more than surface methods is required to raise the corporate performance to acceptable levels.

Following the approach taken in Chapter II a few propositions thought to relate importantly to the practice of management follow:

Management is the critical business discipline.

Management is a susceptible discipline.

Management aims to create three excellences.

Management is a sophisticated discipline.

Management is a reflexive discipline.

Management is a secondary activity.

Management is an intellectual discipline.

Management has social importance.

Management Is The Critical Business Discipline

As has been noted previously, no business survives gratuitously. Survival in a competitive economy results only from deliberate, intelligent, and efficient effort.

Effective management is certainly the precedent excellence, only following which an enterprise can achieve full utilization of its resources and a dependable expectation of survival. No resource can be rich enough or activity brilliant enough to protect a poorly managed enterprise against competitive inroads or self-destruction. Poor management and the wastage of resources are kindred.

Management (in varying degrees of effectiveness) is an inescapable corollary of enterprise. Where two or more people work together the problem of managing arises. Wherever specialized functions join to produce and get something into users' hands, functions must come into being whose tasks are solely to meet the needs of and integrate the producing activities.

This is as true of individuals as it is of groups, of machines as it is of beings. Biological systems, ideally illustrate the managerial role. Even the most primitive multicellular organisms must have cells whose functions serve to control the activities of the whole. Even physical systems, such as computers, must have an executive (management) function of some kind if they are to operate as designed.

The need for management arises in business because working groups are made up of individuals whose actions are not, except in the condition of slavery, completely determinable. Man is idiosyncratic; little in business would get done without there being a function enfranchised to force effort in common directions. And the word force, unpleasant as it is to our ears, is not a bad description of an essential aspect of management. It is that force designed to see that forces of other design perform their allotted functions.

In a free society management arises as a substitute for the coercive force in a totalitarianism society. Interestingly enough, in the latter society the discipline of management does not exist. In an authoritarian state the dessicated shadow of management is called administration.

Before moving on, it may serve a useful purpose to look again at the statement "...management (in varying degrees of effectiveness) is an inescapable corollary of enterprise." The statement is noteworthy because it points to the fact that every business institution - healthy or collapsing, growing or stagnant - is being managed in some fashion.

Managerial personnel and activities at work do not, however, imply that every firm is making or is on its way to profits. Firms can be managed to their deaths, and dying firms are managed on their way to their demise. The impressiveness of management at work - however effective it may be in its observed form - is one of management's most painful problems. The very existence of management often staves off help being requested by or offered to a dying firm. Even defective managing tends to look and sound far better than it is.

Management Is A Susceptible Discipline

Though it is the critical discipline the importance of management is often obscured by the more direct involvements of a firm - such as closing a sale, obtaining funds, changing a product feature. So keen is the awareness of operating requirements in most businesses that management needs are seldom well attended to.

To some, that condition will seem paradoxical because there seems to be almost no end to what is known about managing. But the tremendous disparity between what is known about management and what is practiced has many understandable and some justifiable reasons, examples of which are lack of experience, necessity for making a lesser choice because of lack of resources or time, and the need to compromise in order to maintain coordination. However, the major cause of departing from managerial standards - willfulness - is neither understandable nor justifiable. Many managers tend to do what they want to do rather than what they should do, with no recognition of the difference between the two. This tendency creates in most companies wide gaps between actual and attainable performance.

It is well known that the difference between the best and worst of companies is largely attributable to differences in the quality of management. Yet, few people, including managers - think of management as a true competitive resource. Corporate success is usually attributed to superior products or marketing, or some form of advantage (as patent protection), primarily those who do not recognize the need to subordinate themselves to the self-discipline involved in being an effective manager. It is a fact, however, that companies who have made themselves big with no sacrifice in quality of performance have done so primarily through superior management, even though they may have started with a product, financial, or other advantage over competitors.

It is a wry fact that tangible advantages, such as market, product, financial, or temporal advantages, are immensely important to the firm that possesses them yet can underwrite the destruction of the firm's competitive capacity. Such advantages can loom so large in the view of key personnel they overshadow the need for effective management. One need not look beyond the histories of Ford, Univac, Baldwin-Lima-Hamilton, H.J. Heinz, and other prominent companies that faltered or had to take up new lines of endeavor in spite of having had market, financial, product, or other advantages.

Management Aims to Create Three Excellences

Effective management is wholly concerned with the provision of three excellences. The three are:
- the provision of wanted products
- the provision of lean costs
- the provision of high resource utilization

Taken together, the three embrace every competence and activity a firm needs in order to survive.

For example, making the finest products of their kind serves no purpose if the products are not needed, wanted, or known. Consumers have to be informed about and interest created in the products offered. Thus, effective management is always concerned with market research, transmission of product knowledge, and sales promotion. Providing lean costs also illustrates the pervasiveness of these excellences. It is impossible to create lean costs without being concerned with product design, purchasing, and human factor engineering. Little needs to be said about the last excellence - high resource utilization - since it comes closest to the common understanding of what the manager's job is all about.

Every executive position should be connected somehow to the provision of each of the three excellences. During a lecture in which this view was presented a controller raised his hand and asked, "I can see the point where some executives are concerned. But what's my job got to do with the provision of wanted products? I'm an accountant, not an advertising man!" The lecturer rejoined, "As controller, how can you not be concerned with the provision of wanted products? To provide such products, a great deal needs to be known about what products are selling and who's buying them. Aren't you, as your company's performance information center, in the best position to provide a lot of information on the buying performance of customers by size class, geographical location, user classification, and so on? And as to costs, aren't you in the best position to tell what the average cost of sales' calls, and, perhaps, the return on that cost by customer classed according to purchase volume are?" The controller had to admit the justice of the rejoinder.

Management Is A Sophisticated Discipline

Management is a sophisticated discipline in the sense of having to discriminate nicely between powerful forces and sense finely the timing of actions whose day is about to come. It is sophisticated because it must balance many oppositions, such as getting men both to create and conform, and committing the enterprise while leaving options open. Management is intellectually appealing and demanding, and certainly does not admit to the ham-handed oversimplifications so often embraced by notions of the executive as "leader" and "motivator."

Nothing more clearly highlights the sophistication of the work and problems of management than the interactions that take place between units and functions. These interactions are of vast importance to business effectiveness yet are, in many respects, untouched in modern business. Concepts of involvement, balance, synergism, and the like come in here, and these involve subtleties not easily apprehended by business executives.

On the score of intellectual content, it is obvious to every student of the discipline that management is becoming an increasingly intellectual practice. Certainly the knowledge available to bring to bear on business questions is growing rapidly and at an accelerating rate as is the necessity to make use of it. The company that permits the judgments made on its behalf to be made on a basis that does not include consideration of the best knowledge is playing with its future.

Management Is A Reflexive Discipline

In attempting to make clear the nature of management the discipline has been variously described. Many of the definitions given and taxonomies assayed, for example. "management is planning, organizing, directing, communicating, coordinating," have by design or inadvertently created the impression that management is a directional process that fulfills its purposes in a unilinear fashion.

It is much nearer the truth to describe management as a reflexive, involved process that moves forward only somewhat more than the distance it moves in other directions. In other words, management does its work as much by cycling back and forth between its various components and making, modifying, or remaking decisions as it does through singular, unmodified decision-making.

Planning offers a perfect example. According to functional descriptions of management, planning precedes organizing, directing, coordinating, et al, which, from a very narrow and specialized perspective, may be true. But planning can never operate to the benefit of a company in that fashion. Plans are born to be changed when necessary, and necessities seldom permit plans to be designed in one fell swoop and implemented through directing, controlling, etc., as designed. The more specific (tactical) plans become the more likely they are to be modified through the process of implementation. Feedback and control usually make it necessary to modify or drop the plans adopted, however skillful the planning done.

Management Is A Secondary Activity

The practical meaning of saying that management is a secondary activity is that the business of business is production or service.

The danger of talking about management as the precedent excellence and the key to success in business is that these words sometimes blind us to familiar and well-founded landmarks for sound industrial action. Unbridled interest in management can lead to mechanistic enterprises in which the enforcement of policies, quelling of mistakes, elimination of redundancies, and implementating of organizational ideals become obsessions instead of targets.

Just as industrial enterprise in Western society is a means to an end, management is a means to an end. It follows, therefore, that managing is a secondary activity. It is apparent that an enterprise should be managed only to achieve the best and least costly production and sales (although there are many executives who behave otherwise). Management begins to fail of its purpose when it concerns itself with matters that do not really relate to the conditions of optimum production and distribution.

This point, obvious though it seems, is ignored on a wide scale. A common type is the manager who regards adherence to rules as more important than the job done, who clings to authority when the line is down, who insists on formalities when the emergency is on. The "empire builder" and the "put it through channels" purist are two examples of The-Primacy-of-Management School. They must be made to relearn the lesson that the scope and character of the management effort should be determined by the needs of the enterprise - not by personal wish, management "principle," or anything else.

Management Is An Intellectual Discipline

The environment in which business operates has a heavy streak of irrationality. Nevertheless, the performance of a firm depends greatly on the use of knowledge and deliberateness. In plain words, cognition, calculation, and judgment are equal or superior in importance to business as intuition, impulse, and taste.

This being the case, management is becoming increasingly dependent on empirically based knowledge. But management can never become a science - it is too large, complex, and dynamic a field ever to become directly responsive to anything resembling physical "laws." More precisely, the management field will never become sufficiently static to support the use of experimental methods as the principal means of discovery. Management is an evolving field, the content of which one day will give it an entirely different appearance.

But, the need to understand and control our business institutions better is real and compelling today. As long as management falls short of being a mature science, corporate management must look to reasoning and judgment as much as to factual knowledge as the bases for taking action. But reasoning and judgment cannot function to a manager's advantage until he believes that his world responds to or can be dealt with on an intellectual basis. In short, he must believe the world of business has some predictability, causality, and responsiveness.

That belief has increasing justification as evidenced by the rising use of systems engineering technology in the management process. Though fragments of the technology have been employed for a number of years, the last decade has witnessed a powerful movement in industry toward systems thinking. Not only is this phenomenon seen in the use of computers, in the present preoccupation with management information systems, and emphasis on systems and procedures; it is beginning to be seen in areas that have to date resisted systematization, such as strategic planning, marketing and, even organizational design. It is no accident that the phrase "system Science" has entered the management vocabulary.

Thus, management is moving with noteworthy speed from the intuitive art it has more or less been to a discipline resembling science in many ways. Of course, the scientific method is not broadly applicable to the affairs of management, but many of the attitudes and much of the decision-making technology of science are taking hold in management.

Management Has Social Importance

It has often been said that the success of business depends upon the kind of society we have. But it may make more sense to take the opposite view; success in business may well determine the kind of society we will have.

This is not to say that the business of America is business. But the lessons being learned in business may offer the model for a society in which individuals can live engagingly with decency and satisfaction. If mankind is ever to create a world free of the waste and inefficiency brought on by inflation, depressions, revolution, dictatorship, and war it will have to adopt features similar to many of those of business management.

Of management it can be said that nothing man has created has more effectively provided the means by which men can work togehter toward the accomplishment of common goals. Five thousand years of intensively organized existence - political, religious, military - have not benefitted man greatly, have not enabled him to live his life without destructive tension or with anything near full self-realization. Management may well prove to be the system that will help bring about a world in which man can live fully, without exterior restraint, and in adjustment to his environment.

In our urbanized, industrialized, interrelated, changing and complex society, management may offer the only body of transmittable knowledge which can permit organizations to live and grow, permit people within themselves to feel secure and achieve self-realization, and permit diverse groups to deal with each other effectively. This knowledge is becoming increasingly independent of political-economic structures or cultural influences. Management practices in all countries now have more in common than in difference and seem to be in the process of forcing the creation for the first time of an international language and communications network.

Though engagement in "trade" has always had detractors, managers should recognize that development of the system of cooperation called management in many respects is in the same class as the development of language and ethical standards. When it operates as a directive, coordinating, and integrating force, and not as the nameplate of private philosophy or dogma, management produces - on the largest scale and most consistent basis - justice, equity, consideration, simplicity, and efficiency. It must have been these qualities that moved the eminent English philosopher, Alfred North Whitehead, to write, "A great society is a society in which its men of business think greatly of their functions." It behooves all men to think greatly of the functions of business.

That injunction is not mindless rhetoric or special-interest propoganda. It is both an expression of the universal importance of business and the practical value of the concepts behind the management of business run for the benefit of all concerned.

IV.
ON THE ROLE OF THE MANAGER

The businessman has not fared well in the history of opinions about him. In Wealth of Nations Adam Smith damned him, claiming any social benefits businessmen produce are accidental by-products of their grasping natures. Similar views are harbored by many today, preventing them from seeing the managerial role in a true light.

The manager must view the managerial role realistically if he is to distinguish business problems stemming from deficiencies in managing from those having other sources. To be able to recognize and do something about managerial problems he will have to know a good deal about the role of the manager in terms of its generic and special obligations.

Some propositions thought to relate to the job of the effective manager are:

The role is unavoidable.

The role is difficult.

The role is myth-ridden.

The role involves significant knowledge.

The role should be results oriented.

The role demands self-restraint.

The role requires a philosophy.

The role is solitary.

The Role Is Unavoidable

An enterprise cannot function without its managers. All the material resources in the world will not make a business viable. It is management that blends the men, money, machines, materials, methods, and other resources, and directs the resultant entity toward common objectives.

No social enterprise (which a business certainly is) runs or maintains itself. All businesses are open systems, and require constant adjustment to survive. The adjustments, when they enable the firms in which they are made to survive, are made by persons of special competence - trained managers.

An example of the need for adjustments of the kind only managers can provide is illustrated by what happens to formal organization immediately following its establishment. Organization is subject to something similar to the second law of thermodynamics; as soon as they are established organizational structures tend to run down, to become undifferentiated. They can be kept reasonably close to their designed configurations only by the expenditure of a good deal of effort (which must be balanced against the worth and uncertainties of the plan). Human institutions have decay rates vastly higher than most physical systems. Without management a business would last just long enough for its assets to be hauled away.

The Role Is Difficult

One of the prominent myths in the land has it that the businessman has more control over his affairs than other mortals, that he is the master of all he surveys. Remember the movies of the 30's and 40's? Edward Arnold never walked toward his screenland offices or board room without being totally in command. As he moved through the aisles or corridors he would fire decisions off right and left with easy assurance and everyone within earshot would snap to attention. Yessir!

No picture of the effective manager could be more false. The facts are that the effective manager - as befits a man whose relations with his world fall well short of those of command - is more reflective than commanding, spends more on the discovery of problems than the solving of them, and makes fewer decisions than his subordinates. The effective manager is a much more quiet man than Hollywood ever depicted him to be.

The reason for that is that the role played by the manager is incredibly complex and extraordinarily demanding and cannot be performed adequately by a person who spends the bulk of his time making decisions. Jay Forrester, inventor of the core memory unit of computers, points out that the role is far more difficult than that performed by scientists or any other professional. Therefore, to be played well, the role involves many changes of focus, pace, and activity. Thus, the effective manager at one time or other is initiator, controller, technician, catalyst, guardian, friend, teacher, and, above all, his own person. The effective manager, indeed, is one who has learned to wear many hats. Those who haven't learned stay wielders of legal authority, which is only one among the many forms of authority and the one that provides the smallest foundation to support a significant executive burden.

The Role Is Myth-Ridden

The field of business management is clouded with more than its fair share of myths. One of the more pernicious ones is the notion that the manager is primarily a doer and maker of decisions. The myth is inimical to society's rightful expectations from business institutions and constitutes a limitation on the manager's understanding of his role.

A high proportion of managers see themselves as doers but do not truly regard themselves as responsible for results. They seek to project themselves as high-energy activists but at the same time are careful to lay the grounds for being able to avoid taking direct responsibility for the quality of results. Seeing a good thing through - in a steady, detailed controlled way - is a mark far less commonly encountered than the rush to decide, tell, instruct, and leave projects behind in the search for new ones.

The manager who makes a fetish of being the most active person around and the maker of the largest number of decisions in sight has failed to see that the effective manager is less visible than the people around him. The manager who overshadows the people around him is using no more than a small portion of the capabilities of his subordinates and is, therefore, a waster of his firm's resources.

The Role Involves Significant Knowledge

Each manager is a user of knowledge, and the better he

uses knowledge the more effective he will be. The best of managers are familiar with a wide variety of subjects, some of them quite sophisticated - such as systems analysis, the storage and use of information, and how to deal with conflict.

At the least, successful executives possess three types of knowledge: knowledge of goals, knowledge of methods, knowledge of realities. The first is exclusive to the firm itself; the second is within the firm as well as in its environment; and the third is in the public domain. Each type is essential to high executive performance.

The foregoing statements are not intended so much to point to the fact that management entails a large amount of definitive knowledge as to indicate that managers should act as much as possible on the basis of what is known. Management knowledge has developed so rapidly in recent years and the accumulation has grown so great that most managers have been left behind. The typical manager is ignorant of such subjects as statistical aids to decision making, mathematical models, current findings in behavioral science, management by objectives, and integrated planning. As a result a sizeable gap has developed between what is known about management and what is practiced, even though knowledge of how to manage is becoming a major factor in competition. Another result is that managers have been forced to learn to make decisions without complete knowledge. Good managers have learned to start with facts and, as required by the economics of the situation and availability of information, to mix them with the products of judgment and intuition to form viable conclusions.

One form of knowledge all managers share in greater or lesser degree is that concerning "the odds." This is so true that it is not far-fetched to define management as the practice of applying probability theory to the field of business. It is heuristic in nature, providing guidance in the selection of courses of action whenever objective knowledge is not readily available or cannot be used.

Knowledge, in the empirical sense, is not, of course, always available for use. On the other hand, management never leads from ignorance. One does not "manage" blindly; where facts are lacking one uses fundamental principles such as the propositions of management given earlier.

A vital kind of knowledge too few managers have enough of is knowledge of what is commonly assumed to be the manager's own province: the institution of business. The field of business has outgrown the oversimplifications so long employed in understanding it. Among other things, the social role of the enterprise and the intellectual content of the work of managing were not adequately recognized, with the result that traditional veiws allowed only the most dessicated understanding.

J. W. Gardner said, "If anything is to be accomplished, leaders must understand the social institutions...through which action is acrried out." Too many managers are content to be familiar only with established notions about business without comprehending that companies simply do not work the way most people think. Since institutions can only be modified by individuals, and each company must be modified to survive, it is important that managers acquire deep knowledge of the commercial enterprise.

Perhaps the most important knowledge a manager can have is self-knowledge, a point revealed in the following passage from "Leadership in a Free Society," (Oxford, 1936) by A. N. Whitehead: "In the past slowly developed ways of life possessed inherent stability, and the processes by which this stability was maintained were never explicitly recognized. But progress gives no time for the gradual development of instinctive wisdom, and the price of stability in the future will be the exercise....of a critical self-knowledge."

The Role Should Be Results-Oriented

All managerial jobs should be designed from the point of view of the results desired, not on the basis of assumptions about the work required to achieve the results. In fact, managerial work should not be designed at all. It should be a consequence rather than a deliberate creation. Whatever designing is done should aim at the elimination of work rather than its creation.

Unless that is the case there can be little hope that managers can be held accountable or that sensible standards for managerial performance can be established. If a manager is not held accountable for results, against what can his contribution be measured - against getting to work on time?

However, to design executive positions for results rather

than work is a tough job. Reams of material on management-by
-objectives and results-oriented management come off presses
endlessly - but no company has yet succeeded in designing on
this basis alone. Still, the struggle to define executive jobs in
terms of results rather than specific activities should be entered
into because, if nothing else, it will force attention on the primary
knowledge of a firm's management - the knowledge of what it
wants to accomplish.

The Role Requires Self-Restraint

The point has been made by some observers that the job of
a manager is a comfortable one; that he lives in a world that
pretty much responds to his bidding, that his power to influence
his environment separates him from the bulk of employees who
are the focal points of authority.

This view of the distance between the role of managers and
other employees may be justified by the manner in which the
typical manager uses power. But the view falls wide of the mark
when it is represented as a description of the effective manager.
The latter uses formal authority sparingly, and is better known
when he is described as a person who fulfills objectives by getting
others to direct themselves rather than by being directed.

The managerial role is seductive, and the run-of-the-mill
manager falls easy victim to the privileges and self-opportunities
offered by his position. But the exceptional manager is not similarly affected. He does not use his office to amplify himself.

Managerial genius lies in the man who loses self-conscious-
ness in dealing with a business problem. The truest measure of
the worth of a manager is that his prime aim is to achieve the
highest levels of system effectiveness, not self-aggrandizement.
He is selfless, in the sense that while he knows the system will
reward competence, the fulfillment of systems requirement is
more motivating to him than personal gain. Managers must retain awareness of this fact, because many business problems
have self-service somewhere at their roots. The manager who
goes to Boca Raton in winter to play golf on a plausible pretext
when he should be in Sheboygan on a legitimate problem is an illustration.

<u>The Role Requires A Philosophy</u>

As has been amply indicated in this book, good management decisions don't arise from information alone, however well generated or employed the information may be. Superior decisions are made by executives who have developed coherent philosophies toward their work, toward their firm, toward business in general, and toward society.

It is impossible for enterprise to be successful for long without its managers having a body of <u>convictions</u> to guide their behavior. A philosophy (another name for a system of integrated beliefs) in itself is not enough to assure a well-run company, but no manager can possess in knowledge form everything that goes into making a decision. Decision-making involves not only information and knowledge but common sense, judgment, and "feelings" about a great many future uncertainties concerning which there is little in the form of established knowledge.

The function of management is to determine objectives; determine the alternative means of reaching those objectives; determine which alternative is preferable in terms of available resources, priority of objectives, and degree of risk; determine what problems may result from choosing an imperfect alternative; and prepare the company for dealing with those problems should they arise. Most likely, a decision will be a compromise between what the manager wants, in an ideal sense, and what must and can actually be done. But his responsibility is to select the action that gets the most done, at the least cost, and with the fewest disadvantages.

That is a huge task when an effort to accomplish it thoroughly is undertaken. That the accomplishment can seldom be realized (the manager can seldom spare the time to examine all the information relevant to a decision) does not mitigate the manager's obligation to go as far in that direction as possible. But, since it is a practical impossibility, at least in the world as it is presently constituted, the manager must have something that gives him (and others) the confidence that he has guides in view that are employable in every situation. That confidence can only arise out of possessing a body of fundamentals so pervasive and powerful that it can be called a philosophy.

In building such a philosophy the effective manager chooses

the base of his influence realistically. There are three bases possible today:

Management through property.

Management through power.

Management through fulfillment of needs.

Choice of the first is not rare but no effective manager considers it adequate. Ownership of the means of production is being rapidly eroded as a basis for influence. The most common choice today is to base management on the possession of some form of power as legal authority or (rather naively) personal magnetism. The last choice - basing managerial influence on fulfillment of needs - is the only acceptable one in a world where subordinates have a hundred ways of telling their bosses to go to hell without moving their lips.

And now it is possible to see more clearly the relationships between information, knowledge, and integrated concepts (or philosophy) as they are viewed in their relations to management in this book. Even if the lack of time and applicable experience were not limitations to effective management, the task of managing effectively through information and experience alone has become humanly impossible. The businessman's environment has moved beyond being known through contact alone. The variables have greatly proliferated, time scales have collapsed, technological development rates have enormously accelerated, and the volume of management-relevant information has grown stupendously.

All in all, today's manager is observer to and participant in a circus of activities that defy comprehension through experience and scholarship alone. Relating and deriving meaning from the sounds and sights of it require ideas arising outside exposure to it. Comprehending the environment requires a philosophy; for, without unifying concepts, connections between phenomena cannot be established.

The Role Is Solitary

Because the effective manager has a philosophy, his "style" of managing necessarily is highly individualistic. He is also independent in the sense that he does not need the support of others when he takes a stand. Thus, every effective manager has two qualities among those that mark him for what he is: he has stand-alone capacity, and a synthesizing mind.

The success of any business depends on decision-making of generally high quality that relies mainly upon the manager as an independent being. Only managers with stand-alone capacity can perform well as business decision-makers. Whatever else he is, the effective manager is not derivative; he needs no power more than the force of his own understanding to decide and do well.

However, while he can be relied upon to exercise independent judgment and to "stand up and be counted" when the deepest questions concerning his firm must be answered, his independence is not self-serving nor disruptive. He has an holistic mind - a mind that constantly moves from the particular to the general, from the subjective to the objective, from the "facts" to the full picture. The effective manager tends strongly to think in "wholes."

V.
ON COMMITTING THE ENTERPRISE

A firm's commitments greatly influence the quality of direction and control and, therefore, are major factors in determining the quality of the firm's performance. No firm can be well-managed that does not have worthy commitments. Hence, in companies bent on superior performance committing the firm takes priority over operations both in time and demand upon resources.

There are a number of commitment functions in every company. Planning, usually, is the most visible and certainly is the most important of them, but policies, organization structures, and training programs also shape the future of the firms that establish them. This section of the book will deal only with the planning function.

Propositions that are considered to have importance with respect to it are:

Planning is the foundation of business success.

Sound plans issue from central ideas.

A viable plan is a commitment to action.

Plans cause change.

Planning has the mission of improvement.

Plans should have positive goals.

Plans should be consistent with values.

Effective plans are integrating.

Plans should be company-centered.

Plans must be felt at the operational level.

Plans should be specific.

Plans should be information-based.

Plans should have a timetable.

Plans lay the basis of control.

Plans should have an executor.

Effective planning has unity in time.

Planning should be planned.

Planning Is The Foundation Of Business Success

Planning - in the sense of identifying and establishing worthy, attainable objectives and of correctly proportioning, assigning, and programming use of the human, temporal, physical, and economic resources required to achieve these aims - is critical to business success. Were the environment of business totally gratuitous, totally formless, planning would be wasteful and complicating. But the future is as predictable as it is uncertain. Though precision in forecasting is seldom possible, developments, trends, and choices of action can often be foreseen, and the firm that does not bother to discover them will be more the future's victim than its beneficiary. Planning holds the key to survival in business and, therefore, should be foremost among business concerns.

Saying a company should plan sounds like the ultimate platitude. However, it is simply amazing how few companies behave as if planning has anything to do with business success, and do no planning whatsoever. The ratio of bad to good planning is in the propositions of transporting an elephant by kayak.

If the foregoing is credible it is natural for the question then to arise, how is it possible that American industry has prospered and grown so? The answer must lie in relativity. If the index of perfection is water (specific gravity of one) the existence of water does not keep a steel ball from floating in molten lead. Similarly, the existence of truly effective planning in an environment where most planning is poorly done does not prevent companies that do not plan well from enjoying degrees of business success. Their competitors usually plan as poorly.

An effective company can be defined as one that is constantly in the process of turning established plans into actualities and developing new plans for future realization. This definition, incidentally, harbors a magnificent measure of executive effectiveness. It touches upon the fact that every manager's work divides itself between actualization of plans (goals, strategic plans, operating plans, schedules, and all other statements of corporate intentions) and planning for actualities (committing the company to carefully weighed, selected, and programmed change). Good managers always do some of both (though in varying proportions depending on their jobs) and the absence of one class of activities is a clear sign of deficient managerial performance. The great majority of managers, unfortunately, contribute only to actualization, thereby leaving their firm considerably more subject to environmental influence than any well-run business should be.

The failure of managers to support and contribute meaningfully to planning in their firms has many sources, but the primary ones are that most executives are oriented more toward problem-solving than problem-finding, more toward operations than opportunities, more to doing than thinking. The typical manager prefers the certainties of making decisions about what he sees and hears to the probabilities of making decisions about what he must wait some time to experience. Most managers are most comfortable with instant feedback. Planning, even of the best kind, affords mostly distant satisfactions.

Sound Plans Issue From Central Ideas

The mainspring of an enterprise is an idea. A sound plan cannot be thought to have less.

The most commonly employed measure of business success in a free economy is survival. Remaining in business is usually taken as evidence that a company is fundamentally sound, that none of its ailments is deadly to continuance in business. But sheer survival is not necessarily a sign of health. Every business has capital, a form of output, or market momentum that can keep it going a remarkably long time even when it is dying. Products continue to sell though their heyday is past; salesmen continue to book orders though prices are out of line; profits continue to be shown though investment is not paying off. Many of the signs normally taken to be those of success continue to be shown by companies that are no longer competing healthily. The steam locomotive makers were dead long before their financial statements showed that they were.

The best assurance of business health does not lie in material assets such as capital, plant, or even customers - although these are the gears of the enterprise - but in the driving force of ideas that direct the energies of the enterprise in the direction of clearly defined targets. A business - no less than a man - needs to be in the grip of such ideas (commonly called beliefs and convictions) in order to live successfully.

In every going healthy business the factor of powerful, mutually reinforcing ideas over-shadows all others. Behind any successful enterprise there has been a prime mover in the form of an idea or group of ideas so overpowering that no contrary ideas could survive. That idea or these ideas command obedience, impregnate all activities, and annihilate all contradictory ideas. Ford (low cost, high volume manufacturing), IBM (lower information unit costs), Litton (management is the most important excellence), GENESCO (specialization in everything to wear) are examples of companies arising out of and/or sustained by a compelling idea or group of related ideas.

That businesses are built and sustained by compelling ideas is a popular notion. But it is one that seldom goes beyond lip service. Very few managers ever in their lifetimes engage in searching out and putting to work the life-giving ideas appropriate to their businesses. Yet nothing contributes more to the building of corporate strength than identifying and giving force to the ideas capable of dominating the energies of men. Companies without such ideas are like clocks without mainsprings. Administration untouched by central ideas only goes through motions, it does not move anything.

Plans laid in the absence of moving ideas are like children raised without parental care; their characters tend to be ill-formed and the results they produce uncertain. If anything signals a strong enterprise it is the obviousness of being held captive by an idea or closely-related ideas.

A Viable Plan Is A Commitment To Action

The plainest definition of a plan is that it is a commitment to action. More often than not, planning is a bow in the direction of appearances than to the hard facts of business survival. Too often, a plan is more a statement of good intentions than steely determination.

Actions cannot be taken without using resources. Therefore, no plan is complete without a coupling of assets. In other words, determining "where we are going" (strategic planning) is a waste without determining "how we will get there" (fulfillment planning). Typical business plans fall so far short of this standard that most of them are no more than day-dreams.

The worth of a plan lies in the resources placed against it (including the assignment of personnel responsible for implementing it). The surest sign of a bad plan is discovered when the question, "How much money, time, materials (or other resource) have been set aside for this plan?" yields a negative answer. A bad plan is a sales quota that is not coupled with money set aside for customer or salesman development, a budget that does not have an associated sum for ensuring that it is followed, a market venture without funds allocated to cover the missionary or penetration period, a control designed without the naming of a "controller." A respectable plan always specifies what will be used, when and by whom, to bring about the results the plan calls for.

There is more to the value of committing resources than meets the eye. It is a test as well as a characteristic of a good plan. One of the best ways of checking the practicability of a plan is to ask, "How do we get where we say we want to go?" Manifestly, when the answer is "Don't know" or "Can't tell," you have a plan that ought to be redesigned or dropped.

Plans Cause Change

Because a workable plan is a commitment to action and a commitment of resources, all plans cause change whether they have been designed to bring about change or not. Sound plans cannot be laid to keep things the same.

Plans designed to maintain current conditions inevitably produce alterations in situations they are designed to help retain - because, among other reasons, they activate the machinery of control. Hence, plans <u>always</u> produce change of some kind, sought or unsought.

This point, so simple and unimposing, holds powerful implication for business planners. Two examples are: (1) if you want to keep things as they are leave them alone, and (2) unless you know <u>exactly</u> the kind of changes wanted, don't bother to plan. If you ignore these two injunctions you will lose what you want to keep and become enmeshed in changes you are not prepared for.

It may be said, therefore, that the first measure of the worth of a plan is that it calls for change. In companies that do not plan to change and do not change as planned no planning worthy of the name takes place.

Planning Has The Mission Of Improvement

Since good plans cause change, one measure of a plan's worth lies in the kind of change it seeks. A worthwhile plan always aims at a particular kind of change - the improving of results. Any other kind does not justify the effort and expense planning requires (which are always considerable).

In determining the kind of changes that are worthy of being planned, one starting place is to look at the choices available. In a competitive world a business has three choices: It can:
- do nothing and die
- merely adapt and limp along; or
- innovate and prosper

The third of these, of course, is the only worthwhile choice and the one most managers espouse. But it is astonishing to see the number of companies that reflect only the first two in their actions - among them prominent companies with sound reputations.

But innovation is not necessarily a bridge to improved performance, because it is not an unalloyed competence. In an environment where it is not controlled, made germane and resultful it can be as damaging as it can be beneficial. As gold in the pockets of a suit can either purchase the wearer's wants when in a store or drown him when in water, innovation can lead to business prosperity or extinction. A need exists, therefore, for an instrument through which the creative process (which tends to overreach, be irrelevant, or insufficiently detailed) can be tamed and made applicable. Planning has arisen specifically in response to that need.

Because the improving of results is the only kind of change planning should pursue, it can realistically be regarded as the process through which the generation, protection and amplification of profits is systematized. It accomplishes this through its special ability to introduce change in an orderly, systematic and practical fashion.

In business, final determination of what constitutes an improvement can only be done on a dollar basis. However we view it, business is an economic enterprise, an activity whose existence and survival are predicated in terms of least-cost. Planning necessity, more often than not, is based on vague and/or highly subjective considerations. It is given a solid foundation, however, when it is based on dollars in the form of savings or profits. Necessity, so construed, naturally focuses attention on repetitive, high unit-cost events and major opportunities for improvement (including exploitation of events occurring outside the company.)

Thus, one measure of the worth of a plan lies in the plan's cost. Every plan, regardless of the results it aims at, has a minimum cost to produce. A sound plan is one whose cost is clearly below the dollar amount it aims at producing.

Carrying the point of view a bit further, a measure of worth also lies in the kind of dollars the plan uses or aims for. A good plan never uses resources more badly needed for other purposes, no matter what the plan costs. In other words, good plans never commit the company to smaller risks when larger ones go unattended. For example, a plan to enlarge shipping facilities cannot be a good one when the company's market is going to hell and there is no plan to improve it.

Of course, not all risks can be seen or correctly assessed and planning is limited to dealing with the risks it can identify and cope with (do something about). Accordingly, plans must be laid in the presence of recognition that the stakes in dealing with risks are often higher than predicted. Survival of the company is the highest of all stakes and sound planning never puts this forward except when the alternative, clearly, is business extinction.

If it is true that corporate effectiveness rests on planning then it is probably true that all plans should in some way relate to the improvement of that effectiveness. Hence, it is probably also true that only plans that are necessary should be formed. Oddly enough, this fact, though widely appreciated, leads to a good deal of confusion, because one man's necessity is frequently another man's luxury. If it is agreed that the only acceptable definition of necessity relative to planning is that it is the improvement of effectiveness that confusion disappears.

Plans Should Have Positive Goals

Plans should always aim at accomplishing rather than stopping something. For example, the aim of a good plan is not to put an end to machine idleness but to raise utilization to levels of profitability. Further, a good plan does not focus on closing a plant but putting resources to better use.

The point sounds trivial or, perhaps, excessively subtle, but the point is worthy of consideration for a number of practical reasons. For one, negative plans cost more to implement and control than positive ones because they fail to capture the interest and cooperation of those whose work is affected. For another, they usually lead to counter-productive activities, such as exemplified by the fair amount of time and energy spent in falsifying expense accounts, sales reports, and purchasing necessities. Thirdly, negative plans lead to controls that can only be designed to keep things from happening rather than, as they should be, designed to make things happen.

Planning Should Be Consistent With Values

A very important indicator of a plan's worth lies in its relationships to the values of the company and the worth of those values. No plan has a chance of implementation at tolerable costs, and some cannot be implemented at all, that do not fit in with corporate values.

Values are characterized by the fact that they are behavior-directing. Accordingly, they profoundly affect every business in all its parts including the planning it does. Hence, effective plans must either tie in with existing values or be directed toward the replacement of those values. A worthy goal can be to alter the values in being.

Unfortunately, not many companies are objective about their values. It is not a popular corporate activity to cut into the tissue of daily affairs and lay bare for examination the values at work. Most of the values in a company are poorly visible and some cannot be admitted to. Many are archaic and not a few are hostile to modern views of corporate management.

These statements will sound extreme to some. But their validity can only be tested against facts, and those are not far to be found. The business landscape is strewn with the bodies of companies that have failed or are failing because the values that underwrote or lay in the path of the plans laid were unrealistic or socially unendurable. Every day in this nation another firm of some size goes on the rocks because the values at work chilled the ardor and allegiance of good men and reduced them to wagetakers.

It is important to understand that no company is without values. There are no vacuums in industrial society any more than there are outside. Values are always present to affect the working of every enterprise.

It is impossible to pick up a stockholder's report, organization manual or newsletter without realizing this. It is, in fact, impossible to get a good look inside executive offices without sensing the values of the place. They are expressed in a thousand and one ways: among other things, in the decor, furnishings, office layout and executive dress and manner. Even more important than visible expressions are those which are not immediately apparent to the eye - such as the views management holds about human nature, the purpose of enterprise, the rights of employees to be informed. These are typical of the values which determine executive behavior, the way information is passed around and the manner in which authority is used.

The second thing to grasp about values is that all corporate actions are caused or influenced by values. The values may be progressive and expressed in objectives, plans, policies, training, leadership or they may be self-serving and resident in authoritarianism, personal ambition, group membership. Whatever form they take, values ultimately underlie every action taken and have much to do with what happens to a company.

Since all corporate actions are in one way or another reflections of values and not all actions are beneficial, it follows that values at work in a company are not always good for it. The plain truth is that compelling ideas do not necessarily support worthy, company-centered action. For example, all companies contain groups with their own ideas about what is important in life (and work). The ideas of some groups do not support the objectives or interests of their companies, as illustrated by the fact that groups may establish standards of production far below attainable levels and punish workers who "break the rate." Members of these groups are being directed by values that hurt the enterprise.

Effective Plans Are Integrating

Another measure of the worth of a plan lies in the degree to which the changes it calls for tie in with the changes called for by other plans of the company and how well it contributes to the coordination of basic activities. A worthwhile plan always dovetails with other corporate plans, the prime benefit being that resources, objectives, and activities are made mutually reinforcing.

Probably no quality of effective planning is more important to an enterprise than its capacity for tying these things together; companies are beginning to recognize this, as signified by their growing tendencies to plan for the corporation as a whole rather than for divisions, departments, or sub-units, and to put planning in the hands of specialists. Another sign lies in the fact that demarcations between short and long-term plans are becoming progressively less distinct with some interesting results, such as the relating of budgets more to long-range intentions than to current need.

The integrative qualities of good plans even extend to activities on the wane and activities to be terminated. No activity should "die" in isolation. Planning is the perfect connecting pin between activities and being born, in full vigor, and phasing out.

These points highlight the fact that business planning is essentially hierarchical. Each plan ought to be formed within the framework of a larger plan or to act as the framework of a smaller one. Organizationally, this means, the plans for each unit should be laid within the plans of larger units or as the frame

of reference for the plans of smaller units. It means, managerially, that the plans of each manager should be closely linked to
those of his supervisor(s) and his subordinates. It means, ad-
ministratively, that tactical plans should mesh with strategic
plans and unit plans fit mission plans.

Thus, a real test of the worth of a plan lies in the connection it has with other plans. A plan cannot stand alone (without
connection to other plans) unless it is the genesis of the planning
process.

Plans Should Be Company-Centered

Effective plans are company-centered. That is they are
based upon considerations applying to and arising within this
company and not any other. Sound plans are, in effect, "tailored"
to the specific requirements and capabilities of a particular company. The plans you make, therefore, should be made on the
basis of your company's needs and no other.

Few generalizations with respect to planning are so obvious
or obviated. Fadism, being the touchstone of so much that is
done in the name of up-to-date management, is a common motive
in the planning process. The sudden popularity of organization
planning departments in the middle and late fifties, more as the
result of blind fashion than proven corporate needs, and since
closed down by the companies that formed them, is an example.

Planning Must Be Felt At The Operational Level

Identification of the kind of change that justifies a plan is
fostered by recognition of the fact that companies cannot safely
leave the reaching of their markets to chance. A can of beans
eaten is an appetite filled; a suit of clothes sold is a period of
wearing lost; empty seats in a plane taking off are gone forever.
The company that has not crystallized its intentions and embodied
them in a plan before the foodstuffs are eaten, the clothes put on,
the plane's door closed, loses out.

Therefore, another measure of the worth of a plan lies in
its scope. Effective business plans always have influence beyond the units in which they originate, always affect primary
business functions. Speaking simply, effective plans always

reach down and make themselves felt at the company-customer interface.

Progressive companies recognize this and spare no effort to make their plans useful at the operational level. No pie-in-the-sky for them. Whatever in the enterprise the changes called for by the company's plans are designed to affect, the effects of good plans will be felt - somewhere, somehow, - in the company's market place.

Plans Should Be Specific

Though a sound plan reaches across organizational lines it does not do so by spreading like a fog. A good plan has laser-like qualities; it specifies its target, pinpoints its intended accomplishment in particular and unambiguous terms. Therefore, an additional measure of the worth of a plan lies in its focus.

This is far from an academic or self-evident point. It clearly spells the difference between a plan and a hope (the latter being the best name for many business "plans"). It reminds us that plans are poor devices for creating general conditions. This point, in turn, reveals that plans cannot be effectively used for dealing with such broad organizational aspects as attitudes, morale or "climates."

Such aspects of the total enterprise are, without question, deeply influenced by the kind of planning a company does. But they are not fit objectives of the planning process because their relationships to productivity cannot be clearly seen, much less described. The objectives of good plans, on the other hand, can always be defined in one sentence.

Plans Should Be Information-Based

A sure measure of the soundness of a plan lies in the stuff of which it is made. Because good plans are company-centered and specific, a plan should always visibly bear the imprint of factual information.

When we think of planning, qualities of imagination, ambition, creative thinking and optimism spring to mind. The necessity of these in planning cannot be questioned. Less frequently, however, do we recognize the equally vital planning element -

knowledge - without which planning becomes an exercise in speculation. And, in this connection, we are not only talking about knowledge upon which to base plans but also knowledge of how to use knowledge in the planning process!

One view of the manager is that he is a fellow who makes things happen. This is fair enough if we also understand that he makes things happen because he:

    a. is not satisfied with present results;
    b. intends to improve on them, and
    c. works systematically to implement the intention.

Adding a, b, and c to the preceding definition immediately raises the work of the manager to that of an employer of knowledge. The manager is a person who makes things happen because he knows recent performance, knows wherein improvement was possible, knows the means available for making improvement, and knows the benefits likely to flow from using the means. The manager who makes things happen in the interest of the company has considerable knowledge of the state of his company, the general economy and the discipline of the management.

Because the manager is an intensive user of knowledge, knowledge-amplifying tools such as mathematical techniques, econometric models and computers are being increasingly employed in planning - especially in such areas as forecasting, facilities planning, marketing profitability analysis, and determination of alternative investment choices. Evidence that this orientation is on the increase is reflected by the fact that many companies are discarding objectives by edict in favor of goals arrived at by deduction and analysis.

As far as knowledge of how to use knowledge in the planning process is concerned, the subject could fill a book. The subject can be summarized in a few general propositions, however, which go something like this:

    - Meaningful planning begins in knowledge of the present position, condition and opportunities of the business.
    - It proceeds in the knowledge that most available information is historical and probabilistic.
    - It takes place with the knowledge that costs permit the use only of truly relevant information.

- It is facilitated by the knowledge that human experience and judgmental capacity can be productive sources of planning input.
- It is refined by the knowledge that basing a plan on facts does not necessarily make it workable (i.e., acceptable).

Plans Should Have A Timetable

Because every business in our society must perform in accordance with economic principles it follows that its gauges of performance are things that indicate measures of accomplishment over time, such as rates, productivity, and similar yardsticks.

It is insufficient that plans specify results, however finely they do so. They must, to be complete, also stipulate "by when." Sound plans are sufficiently complete to make the designating of checkpoints possible, so that progress in attaining results may be monitored.

Plans Lay The Basis Of Control

Though this is a broader and "looser" requirement than the preceding two, it is no less vital. What it means, basically, is that plans should be laid only where control can be exercised. Where adherence to the plan cannot be enforced and corrections to unacceptable or excessive deviations cannot be made, planning is a waste of effort.

Part of the planning job, therefore, is consideration of the types and extent of control required for the plan's realization. Where the controls cannot be clearly visualized - beware of laying plans.

Plans Should Have An Executor

The surest way of achieving the results sought by a plan is to assign responsibility for attaining them to one man. Excellence in a plan only makes its implementation easier, it does not make it more likely. The best of plans come to naught left to their own devices.

This requirement greatly complicates the planning process,

because it forces planners to deal with many questions besides those directly involved by the objectives of the plan. Delegation of authority is an example. But it also adds greatly to the effectiveness of the process because it makes planners think things through and be thorough.

No requirement more than this better shows that plans are not sound simply in terms of their intrinsic worth. There will be times, in fact, when a given plan will prove impractical even where the objectives seem realistic and attainable, because "secondary" consideration makes them uneconomical or too disruptive to organize.

Effective Planning Has Unity In Time And "Space"

Perhaps the single most important idea about planning is that it is contributory primarily when it is done as a whole, as an entity, as an unbroken process. In short, planning is productive only when it is done to completion.

Proof of this assertion lies in the fact that it is impossible to find a single item called a plan that embraces all of the features associated with plans. In other words, the terms plan or plans arc the names of a class of objects each member of which differs in some way from all other members of the class. In effect, planning is a class name and not the name of any singular device used to shape the future. There are strategic plans, technical plans, objectives, policies, long-range and short-range plans; but no one of these can be taken as a generic definition of a plan. Thus, it appears reasonable to say that planning is a process that nears completion only when the many kinds of things comprising plans are utilized on an integrated basis.

Effective planning is time-consuming, expensive, and probably much too complex for any but a specialist to execute.

Planning Should Be Planned

A sound plan is never a gratuitous event, it emerges as a result of calculated intentions through the agency of skillfully designed procedures.

A main reason the cost of planning has received so little attention is that planning has usually been regarded as a non-linear activity, a unique activity, an activity that ends with the production of a plan. This is a dangerous and costly view. If it is true that business planning is critical to business survival and progress, it is equally true that the planning must be organized and run as a continuous operation.

Planning also suffers from fuzzy organizational thinking. Because all managers have something to do with the production of plans, planning is often left to "somebody else," "somewhere else." In other words, planning more often than not is an amorphous function with no organizational locus. This is an absurd condition! True enough, every manager has planning responsibilities and his work benefits in the degree to which he develops skill on contributing to the building of sound and realistic plans governing his and the activities of those he directs. But, planning seldom has a chance of success where it takes place outside a system of tight planning procedures followed by persons with precisely defined planning responsibilities. Thus, the idea that every manager should produce the plans affecting his area of cognizance is not necessarily a good one. Planning should, generally speaking, be centralized and performed (or at least, controlled) by specialists.

Studies bear this out by revealing that corporate planning is becoming more formal (even though less complicated.) As noted earlier, planning is becoming increasingly more systematic and strategic - trends that have been made possible by the establishment of procedures assignments and schedules. The corporate planning office is becoming a common feature throughout all but the smallest classes of business sizes, bearing testimony to the fact that planning is increasingly coming to be viewed as a formal and specialist function.

The phenomenon of the corporate planning office owes existence not only to having an identifiable location but to being plugged into well-defined channels of communication as well. In other words, planning must have a clear organization position fed by prominent informational pipelines. Only in situations where it is richly connected within a soundly engineered communication network can planning function effectively and efficiently. Where planning does not occupy such a position it is uninformed and mute.

Because planning is the most poorly performed of all the leading business functions the value of any light that can be shed upon the process is beyond question. In the hope of such illumination sections have been placed in the appendix taken from a planning document prepared by the author for a nearly billion dollar a year corporation. The excerpts have, of course, been modified to prevent identification of the firm. But the points of universal application have been left as originally stated and the reader interested in the planning process may find them worth reviewing.

VI.
ON SECURING INTENDED RESULTS

Plans are implemented through the compliance functions - particularly those of controlling and directing. Though the two seem very dissimilar, they have much in common. They share responsibility for bringing about the results envisioned in the plans each company lays.

Every phase of business life is affected by controls. But in spite of their importance there is a wide lack of understanding of what makes a good control as opposed to a poor one. In an effort to make clear some of the characteristics of effective controls the following propositions are presented:

Controls should be specifically needed.

Controls should focus on accomplishment.

Controls should be enactable.

Controls rest on measurability.

Controls should be kept simple.

Controls should operate infrequently.

Controls should result in corrective action.

Controls should operate by comparing.

Controls should be strategically located.

Controls should have a controller.

Controls should not survive plans.

Controls Should Be Specifically Needed

Probably the general state of no body of business mechanisms offers a more patent contradiction of the spirit of management than that of controls. Most controls in business are bad - not only because they are defective in concept and grounding - but also because they are illusory. Their very existence offers the appearance of being on top of things. The fact is, the administrative landscape is strewn with controls that serve no useful purpose whatever.

The first step in the establishment of sound control is to make sure that the control being contemplated is required in fulfilling the terms of clearly stated objectives. Controls should not be made to stand alone; effective controls are occasioned by plans in one form or other. Hence, it is useful to ask of a control under consideration: "What is it this control is supposed to help make happen?" If some kind of accomplishment cannot be found control design should stop at that point.

The safest course with respect to controls is to make the specifying of controls part of plan development. It seems eminently sensible, therefore, to have each plan identify and describe the controls needed.

Controls Should Focus On Accomplishment

As plans should have positive aims, so should controls. Control should be exercised not so much to keep things from happening as to make the "right" things happen. Realization, not repression, is the highest purpose of controlling.

This is not an academic point. A firm with mainly negative controls clearly has a doleful view of human nature and no understanding of where it wants to go. Further, negative controls are psychologically repressive, and they obscure the higher aims of the business as well as inviting evasion by employees. Controls that invite evasion can lead to greater losses than would occur if they didn't exist.

What is worse, negative controls - simply because they exist - can lead to the assumption (with attendant, misleading comfort) that control objectives are being met. This is false; not only do negative controls not make good things happen, they seldom prevent bad things from taking place.

Controls Should Be Enactable

It is all too commonly held that the principal tests of the feasibility of a control lie in the ability to design and install it. This view is acceptable only if the boundary of control is drawn at the point of getting it on the books. But a control is an operating device and is not defined by the procedures that make it up. One sign of an ill-conceived control is that it is inoperable.

Remember prohibition? The plan was to eliminate drinking. Because the controls established could not enforce the law not only was drinking not eliminated but the foundation for the world's largest criminal operation was laid.

Therefore, only controls that can operate (relative to objectives) should be established. The astute manager recognizes that exceptions that cannot be acted upon constitute avoidance of planning intentions and cause erosion of control. Worse, it diminishes the likelihood of the plan behind the control being successfully implemented.

Controls Rest On Measurability

To be enactable, controls must be capable of being activated on the evidence of deviations from intentions. To be so capable requires a method of discrimination. Thus the evidences of deviation must be measurable in their degree of variance. That requires a yardstick of some kind. Ideal yardsticks are always quantitative in character.

While it is not always possible to find such yardsticks, managers should be wary of departing too far from them. Controls diminish rapidly in effectiveness, both organizationally and psychologically as yardsticks become inexact. When the yardsticks cannot be quantified, the controls have no basis of discrimination and cannot avoid, therefore, being triggered by every variation - however small.

Controls Should Be Kept Simple

If it is true that controls should be invoked only that are necessary, it is also true that controls should be no more complicated than necessary. They should be made no more elaborate than needed to detect and correct significant deviations from plans. Testing for deviation significance is a good guide for control design. A control that is activated by small variations is already too complicated.

Controls depend, of course, for their working upon information that arises out of the activities controlled. This kind of information is called feedback. A control receives the energy it uses in discriminating between a significant and an insignificant deviation from the activity it is set up to govern and only operates when systems output does not compare acceptably with the performance desired. A familiar example of control based on feedback is the household thermostat; as the heat provided rises past a predetermined comfort point it actuates a thermocouple that shuts the heat off.

Four steps are always taken when establishing a successful control. The steps are:

1. developing effective standards
2. setting them at strategic points
3. creating feedback for performance comparison
4. setting up the machinery for correcting destructive deviations

Controls Should Operate Infrequently

It is popular to think that a good control works full time. This notion is untrue; a good control only operates intermittently. No control of human behavior can operate constantly. To do so completely vitiates the purpose and exhausts the objects of the control.

If it is accepted that business controls are in the form of system, then a number of systems engineering principles applies to them, knowledge of which assures the manager of sound guides in designing controls. The more important of these principles, loosely stated are:

1. Effective controls use no more of the primal energy (the activities controlled) than is needed to assure that the activity monitored accomplishes its task as intended.
2. While in force, effective controls are energized continually but "operate" infrequently.

3. Controls can operate infrequently only when activated by exceptions.
4. Exceptions come into being when control sensory threshholds are set that are exceeded only by actions that threaten to destroy the objectives set.

Controls Should Result In Corrective Action

Though a control should not operate often, when it does a change of some kind should result. The surest sign of a defective control is that nothing overt happens.

Control does not end with detection or the noting of exceptions. It is only completed with the taking of corrective action leading to the elimination of non-productive (vis-a-vis the objective) effort.

Controls Should Operate By Comparing

It has been noted that effective and efficient control requires the adoption of objective, accurate, and suitable standards of measurement. But that is not the whole story. Effective controls always contain the means for making comparisons between what is taking place and the standards. On this basis, attention should be given primarily to the definition and detection of exceptions.

Only large variances should be controlled. The great bulk of repetitive activities (and these are the ones to be most carefully controlled) vary in some degree from the standard. To act on every variance is to invite economic disaster; controls must - if they are not to eat you out of house and home - operate only when a variance appears that threatens to prevent the established goal from being reached. Finding the degree of variance that can be tolerated is a cost-critical task that must be done with considerable nicety if the control to be set up is to serve the purposes of the business and not vice versa. If this can't be done, forget it!

Controls Should Be Strategically Located

It is impossible to control processes throughout their operation; control must be exercised at points (interfaces) where change occurs.

Just as measurements can only take place at points, so controls can only be actuated at points, junctions, interfaces. This being the case, the best place to insert control is where something is likely to happen, where change of some kind occurs, for example at the point a purchase order becomes an invoice, when a petty cash voucher becomes an outlay, when a picked order becomes a shipment.

The idea of creating feedback must be made explicit. Controls are far more often than not set up as definitions of what is undesirable without being given the mechanism of information generation, processing, and utilization that enables the controls to operate. Thus, most controls are verbal and little else. A control with so insubstantial a character usually requires a sizable portion of an employee's time to make it work. Very wasteful!

As a corollary to the system requirements of control it needs to be suggested that controls should be located advantageously from the organizational viewpoint. The exercise of control should not place strain on organizational relationships; make sure that the machinery of control and the organization are compatible.

Controls Should Have A Controller

Every control associated with management action requires a human being as part of the control loop. Management controls can never be fully automated; God help the company that lets a computer make credit decisions.

Failure to observe this simple rubric has cost many companies customer goodwill, a good share of their profits. At the time of writing this book the author gave up a credit card he had held for over ten years and had used heavily (to the profit of the issuer) because he got tired of being warned that his "account was coming under serious review" when he had an unexcelled credit record. Without entering into further detail, the reason the credit card company lost his significant business is that no review of computer output was made by a person who could make a judgment as to the propriety of a warning or other form of notice that could alienate a subscriber. Hence, if a management control is to be instituted be sure to include a human being in its circuitry.

Controls Should Not Survive Plans

As long as a plan is in the process of being actualized (that is, causing action) the associated control(s) should be continued. When the plan is realized or abandoned the control(s) should be discontinued.

Unfortunately, most controls long outlast the plan (formal or otherwise) that it was set up to help actualize. A true sign of an "unhealthy control" is long life and no regular review.

Most laws on the books of whatever government are unenforced complicating the process of law enforcement. Similarly, old controls lying about constitute hazards to the attainment of effective management. Before lean and facilitating management can be instituted, the junk of old controls and other remnants of administrative muddle-headedness will have to be cleaned out.

VII.
ON SELECTED MATTERS

In this section are a number of propositions selected as much for their illustrative as their intrinsic value. They have been selected both because they are examples of the kinds of propositions the manager should recognize in addition to those in the previous sections and because they are useful in themselves.

The term "examples" can be taken to imply two things: (1) there are far more propositions that can be formed that hold value for the individual manager than can possibly be covered here and, (2) the propositions given here are thought to be correct statements of management realities but are not claimed to so proven. In short, the propositions are, for the author, still in the process of being finally formulated.

There are in the next few pages the following propositions:

The performance of every firm can be improved.

Every decision in business affects the capacity to survive.

Survival and growth are critically intertwined.

Survival capacity hangs on liquidity.

To survive every firm must seek to grow.

Growth amplifies resources.

The door to survival and growth has three keys.

Every business has two kinds of problems.

All business resources are economic.

Manpower is the most important resource.

Achieving high manpower utilization is the most difficult managerial task.

Manpower should not be hired for life.

Managerial productivity is indicated by the use of time.

Understanding and mobility are critical to high productivity.

Management skill is not technologically based.

Freedom has economic value.

Conformity is a business requirement.

Authority is a resource.

Information is what resolves uncertainty.

Possession of information bestows power.

Managers must develop themselves.
Management should not repress conflict.
Willfulness is the prime barrier to exceptional performance.
Business success is founded on the unusual.
Organize for unknowns as well as knowns.

The Performance of Every Firm Can Be Improved

Business institutions, like most living things, are hardy. Companies can tolerate almost any number of mistakes stemming from honest efforts to improve their performance. It is hard to kill a firm by really trying to help it do better. That quality makes it possible in any company to pursue improvement actively. Were the situation otherwise, the care that would have to be taken in introducing change would bring the change process to a standstill. No company could survive that.

Even assuming a company can be tuned to perfectly execute its assumed tasks - a poor assumption - it is inconceivable that such perfection could be more than momentary. The pace of business life is such that it must be recognized that the corporate environment is in constant flux. In that case, no change can have prolonged effectiveness. It follows, therefore, that there is every likelihood that improvement can be made in any enterprise wherever determined efforts are made to secure it.

Even the best run of companies is far from what it can potentially be, and the firm that does not make fulfillment of that potentiality a principal aim will always stand in the shadow of what it might have been.

Every Decision in Business Affects The Capacity to Survive

Every business decision in one way or another either contributes to a firm's ability to survive or damages that ability.

Reflection will show that every action in the universe either contributes to the maintenance of some aspect of its current state or changes it. Take the simple acts of eating and drinking; taking on a meal or drink either does no more than replenish bodily needs or it does less or more than that. If it does less than replenish bodily needs, it impairs the body's survival capacities; if it does more, it results in such conditions as obesity. Similarly, business decisions either feed survival capacities or damages them. There are no alternatives.

The idea seems to be on the simple-minded side. Perhaps it is, but it is impossible to deny that every decision made consumes resources in the making and in being implemented. Whatever the objective of the decision, then, survivability is affected one way or the other. Decisions made but not implemented and decisions implemented that do not at least return as much of resources as used damage survivability; decisions that pay back more in the way of resources than used amplify survivability.

To that rubric, of course, must be added another dimension -- time. It is insufficient to posit the balance between resource consumption and restoration alone as the critique by which to measure decision performance. It must also be said that it is the relations between consumption and replenishment over the lifetime of the decision that determines whether the decision hurts or helps survivability.

Hence, managers should make no move that does not favor their firms' capacities to stay in business. Risks - as any business decision necessarily entails - should always be examined from that point of view. A risk that does not have every appearance of enhancing survivability most likely will damage it.

In spite of the impact every business decision has on survival capacity, how often is an impending decision examined for effects beyond the immediate? How often do managers ask what the effects of decisions they are about to make on their firm's resources will be? The answer must be, "seldom."

Survival and Growth are Critically Intertwined

Growth strategies may appear to be exceptions to the proposition that every business decision either contributes to a firm's capacities to meet its commitments or it takes away from those capacities. However, if the proposition is true, then a decision that does not contribute to a firm's survival capacity is a bad business decision - whatever its intrinsic worth may be.

Measures for growth, particularly, should be examined for their effects on the firm's survival capacity. Firms typically pin hopes for survival on growth without asking how the growth measures affect survivability. There is nothing intrinsically good or safe about striving to get bigger. There is much in the way of managerial wisdom to examine growth proposals far more closely than maintenance ones. Growth proposals often lead to steps that involve significant portions of a firm's worth and command priorities in the use of resources. The only sound growth decisions are those that also meet the firm's survival requirements.

It is quite possible for an idea that is marvelously innovative, complete, intelligent, and intriguing to be disastrous to the company that undertakes it. Ideas in business, like love affairs, flourish in their proper time, otherwise die. Henry Ford's success, for example, can be as much attributed to timeliness as to inventiveness. The automobile was a well-established vehicle when he came on the scene. Had he tried the same idea 20 years earlier or later, his name would have been as forgotten as those of the legion of men whose ideas were out of step with their times.

Hence, survival and growth needs of an enterprise are both served by decisions that promote expansion for sound business reasons. On the other hand, decisions that promote growth for its own sake inevitably reduce the ability of the firm to survive. Therefore, for a firm to stay alive the measures for growth must also meet the firm's survival requirements.

Survival Capacity Hangs on Liquidity

Make no mistake about it; whatever you do must not be allowed to impair your firm's survivability. If there is any constant close to the bone of business it is that which expresses the need to maintain resources at levels needed to sustain the firm's ability to exploit its opportunities. This is another definition of liquidity; the name for access to resources that allow fast action to be taken.

It is unreasonable to expect either resources or environments to remain constant. It is not incumbent upon a firm to keep sales up or growing, or to keep its resources at a constant dollar value. The Great Depression taught the futility of that. But every firm that wants to stay in business must maintain its abilities to seize and use its opportunities, and that, in turn, depends on its abilities to lay its hands on its resources. On that survival and growth both hand.

Turn this around and you get another guideline for corpo-

rate survival: make no commitments that can overtax the firm's resources. Thus, decisions that go beyond helping a firm meet survival requirements should not be couched solely in terms of getting bigger; a growth decision can consist in the aim to get smaller _if_ (as is possible) it results in an increase in corporate resources. Survival is based more on liquidity than profitability; and many a firm has grown to its death because it bought sales volume at the expense of the ability to pay its way.

To Survive Every Firm Must Seek to Grow

If any proposition takes on the aspect of a bromide this one does. But, as has been stated before about similar propositions, its implications are fascinating.

Though growth decisions are more dangerous (entail more risk) than maintenance ones, every firm should seek to grow nonetheless, because growth brings about improvement in a firm's survival capacity. Growth should be an objective because resources are subject to constant erosion. No resource can be counted upon to last indefinitely.

Only sound growth, however, can benefit a firm. Therefore, growth should be sought only with the aim also of improv ing survival capacities. To grow for other reasons: pride, p vate gain, or (as is so often done) simply for the sake of gr subjects the firm to unwarranted risk. To grow as a re filling a gap in the product line, to round out pricing, to the use of salesmen's time, to reduce distribution cos id, but to grow simply to get bigger is in the same ca ling one's weight for no other purpose than to get Suicidal!

Growth Amplifies Resources

The only viable definition of growth creases the availability of resources - r such as height, volume, weight, profi can be achieved with no increase in v

This definition yields some ne of looking at business. For exa view growth as occurring throu

71

pruning unprofitable customers, curtailing LTL shipments, drop ping fading products) or as occurring in non-financial ways (e.g., developing latent skills, recruiting high potential personnel).

The last point touches upon the fact that corporate resources are immensely varied and are not purely financial in character (although they are in influence). Growth, therefore, can take place in an infinite variety of ways, growth in physical resources, probably being among the less important these days. Human resources certainly cast light on this matter. The fact that human resources accounting has sprung into being proves that.

The Door To Survival and Growth Has Three Keys

For a company to grow without impairing its survival capacity is a handsome accomplishment. The feat, if it is to be the product of deliberate action (which it almost always has to be), requires for its accomplishment some fundamental changes in the traditional way of looking at business. At the least, it requires shifts in thinking of the business from the owner's to the customer's viewpoint (externalization), from the subjective to the objective (rationalization), and from conducting the business in a fluid, informal to a more structure, formal way (institutionalization).

By externalization is meant shifting the basis of decision making from the perspective of owners to that of customers (actual and potential). Years before consumerism came into prominence, companies that enjoyed outstanding success were companies that paid a lot of attention to the outside world, particularly to customer needs and competitor behavior. The companies that did not, died, as exemplified by -

- the great steam locomotive companies, not one of which saw diesel-electric power as a competitive threat
- Packard, which valued its engineering accomplishments more than drivers' satisfactions.

nly have individual firms died, but so have entire industries. ailroad will not die as an industry, but it is almost certain will die as a privately-owned one. Only the most gro distortion of free-economy views can save it from being ized.

rationalization is meant shifting from opinion to infor-

72

mation-based action, from intuition to reasoned judgment. It means shifting from managerial primitivisms, such as thinking that the key to success is to pay as little as possible for everything, to the recognition that business is a complex affair with a high intellectual content. That phrases like game plan, trade-offs, and management by objectives have come into business language shows that this viewpoint is being increasingly recognized. Seat-of-the-pants management, management by impulse, must give way to deliberate, informed, reasoned management.

By institutionalization is meant shifting from ad-hoc, laissez faire, elitist management to management by plan, control, and adjustment - none of which is possible without structuring, formalizing. The story of Jethro and Moses told in the Old Testament illustrates the need for institutionalization. Individual genius, devotedness, perception must be universalized, must be reflected in every aspect of the institution. That, probably, explains why Hitler succeeded in making a nation of less than 100 million withstand nearly a billion people for four years.

Every Business Has Two Kinds of Problems

All business problems can be put into two classes: those that are necessary and those that are unnecessary. In other words, business problems are either consequences of being in business or they are not. Proportions between the two constitute the measure of a company's condition. A healthy business has mostly necessary problems; a "sick" company has mostly unnecessary ones.

Though almost any business executive will agree with the foregoing statements, it is rare for an executive to pause and ask whether the problem he is dealing with, like the war-time trip, is really necessary. Yet, it is commonly thought that one of the most important functions of an executive lies in the elimination of waste. If that view is correct, an awful lot of executives are wasting their time solving problems that shouldn't exist in the first place. Redundant decision-making, "reinventing the wheel," in many companies is the greatest waster of their most precious asset - managerial time.

Why executives do not behave more intelligently is difficult to answer. Perhaps one of the main reasons is that a high percentage of businessmen persist in thinking that managing is very much like trading, an economic activity offering managers little to measure their value by except the number of transactions (problems) they can handle in a given amount of time. How unintelligent! The wise executive measures his effectiveness by the number of problems he succeeds in not having to handle. The ineffective executive spends a good deal of his time solving problems. The effective executive spends a good deal of his time preventing the wrong kind of problem from arising. The high-volume problem-solver, though the darling of the business myth perpetrators, is a real troublemaker.

A reason why many managers waste time solving unnecessary problems is that they have not learned their managerial ABC's. They are not remotely aware that the fewest number of problems (A problems) cause the greatest losses while the largest number of problems (C problems) cause the smallest losses. Most managers have never learned to measure their effectiveness in terms of what they don't do rather than what they do. Most managers have a Pavlovian responsiveness to problems; present them with a problem and they will automatically try to solve it irrespective of its reality, size, or costs.

To do his job properly the manager must have a basis for recognizing which problems he should solve and which he should sidestep. There are many tests of the "value" of a given problem, but the best way to distinguish between a necessary and an unnecessary problem is to ask whether solving the problem will make any immediate difference in the company's asset position. If the answer is negative ask a new question: "If nothing is done now will the problem disappear for good?" If the answer to this question is yes, forget the problem. If the answer is no, a new question arises: "What will be needed to keep the problem from arising again?" If the answer is that move "x" or "y" will eliminate the problem permanently make the move or moves. If nothing can be done to keep it from cropping up in the future, you're right back where you started; you've got a problem that must be solved.

The real problems of a company are always in some manner the consequence of being in the business it is in; e.g., the problem issues from the necessities of meeting price and product competition, of securing properly skilled workers, of obtaining the lowest cost material with the required properties. The other problems are always in some manner the result of poor managing.

If management is, among other things, the systematic practice of economy of means, it follows that manpower must be treated as economically as the other resources of a business. The key to using manpower efficiently is to see it works primarily on necessary problems. This means that every business should spend the effort necessary to find, identify and root out the false problems that waste its executives' time.

All Business Resources Are Economic

Whatever their specific form, (for example, material, ideational, individual, social) every resource in and of a business has profit and loss consequences in the way it is used. Accordingly, each resource should be regarded as being economic in character, and should be utilized so as to produce the best financial return.

This view is not readily accepted when extended to certain resources - such as information. But, the secret to using that resource effectively is to treat it as one having profound economic consequences.

Manpower Is The Most Important Resource

The quality of human contribution in the short and long range is the primary determinant of a company's destiny. Therefore, of all the excellences in business practice, excellence in the employment of human resources has primacy in the building of sound and continued profitability. Before financial or physical resources can be used to the best advantage people have to be employed to the best advantage.

It has always been true that the company that maintains a perpetual objective of the aim to excel in the employment of its personnel will enjoy a significant competitive advantage in whatever field it operates. It follows, therefore, that the company that fails to aim at creating this excellence now stands in the presence of growing dangers because the capability for dealing economically with the immense complexities of a large-scale manpower information field is rapidly approaching the status of an accomplished fact. Possession of this capability will greatly diminish other forms of advantage in the hands of competitors who do not have the same capability.

Any company has a long way to go before it has the capability of making the best use of its manpower resources. Since a company's relative position in the industrial world will be vitally affected by the relative speed with which it incorporates the advances being made in manpower management, it is in the greatest of the company's interests, therefore, that it make these advances part of its own manpower management capabilities as soon as possible.

Though it is widely acknowledged that skill in the employment of people determines the skill with which other forms of business resources are used, it is not possible to find rigorous application of this principle in business anywhere. Up to now, the employment of human beings has been a blind art, mainly because people are not fixed assets and the means for maintaining intimate contact with a dynamic, multitudinous resource has not until now approached technical and economic feasibility.

Because of the lack of this contact, companies, generally speaking, know far more about their physical assets than about their people. This is as true of the biggest and best of companies as it is of smaller and less efficient ones. In fact, the smaller company, by its greater intimacy of personnel relationships, often scores higher marks in this area.

Achieving High Manpower Utilization Is The Most Difficult Managerial Task

Of all the resources needed for accomplishing business purposes, none presents greater diffuculty in being utilized efficiently than the manpower resource. No achievement ever cost more for the work done to solve the technological problems than to provide, administer, and motivate the human resources needed to create the achievement. The failure to reach major objectives most often can be traced to the prime managerial displacement - that of devoting the least amount of effort to the most important and difficult task (effectively utilizing manpower).

Manpower is a unique resource. Of all the resources of business enterprise not one calls for the amount or varieties of knowledge required to use it wisely as does manpower. Therefore, skilled management of human resources is founded upon the development of a large, accurate, and comprehensive body of relevant information. The body must be comprehensive because manpower cannot be understood in one dimension of time or behavioral pattern. Its maximum value, for example, may not reside in what it can do now but what it can do in the future. Knowledge of what a company's manpower may be capable of requires knowledge of what it had done. As capable as it is of free will it is capable of being predicted. Knowledge of manpower as a group may yield little knowledge of manpower individually.

No company has adequate information about manpower today. This fact, more than any other, describes the potential inherent in solving the information problem as it relates to manpower management. But the means for building an adequate information system is rapidly forming with the advent of large numbers of general purpose computers; the building of banks of detailed information about personnel is rapidly becoming possible.

Manpower Should Not Be Hired For Life

There is a compulsion in business to hire personnel in the longest range terms. Succumbing to this temptation leads to tremendous mistakes, such as the rejection of older men (whose experience is often deeper and more varied and needs more modest than those of younger men) and passing over the candidacy of young men looking for acceleration in their careers. The only true measure of the worth of a hiring does not rest in potential years of employment but production over time. Any man is worth hiring who can produce results with value exceeding the costs of becoming indoctrinated.

There is, of course, a need in every firm for human excellence but, because excellence is by its very nature a rarity, there is also need for turnover (paced so as to get enough turnover to exit spent manpower and bring in fresh thinking). The ideal situation, of course, is one where the costs of recruitment and indoctrination are incurred only once every six or seven years for a given position. But that is strictly an ideal and cannot be expected to prevail for many positions in a firm that is truly growing.

Managerial Productivity Is Indicated By The Use of Time

A production worker's productivity can be measured by the number of pieces he turns out, as can the productivity of most other members of the firm. But the productivity of managers is not nearly so measurable, because the results they produce are produced through others and as often appear in the future as in the present.

Since immediate results cannot be a reliable measure, looking for measures of current managerial productivity leads to indirect measures. A leading indicator of manager's productivity resides in their use of time. No effective manager is careless in his use of time. He recognizes that it is his principal resource in getting things done, and is careful in selecting objectives upon which to spend time.

Using time effectively requires of managers that they have:

a) knowledge of the nature, aims, status, and prospects of the firm;

b) appreciation of the distinctive work of management; and

c) understanding of themselves as individuals.

Few managers have anything near all three forms of cognizance. Every effective manager has fair knowledge of each, but they are in the minority. Most managers know, at best, a little about one or two. The typical manager is, therefore, a poor user of time.

Signs of the lack of the three forms of knowledge are:

a) an endless appetite for information;

b) excessive use of power;

c) constant need for personal approval.

Ineffectual managers exhibit the three characteristics to greater or lesser degree.

In respect to the three forms of awareness, effective managers have something similar to the following realizations:

1. They realize that having all the information relating to the typical managerial decision is far less important than having the key information (seeking the former gets in the way of getting the latter).

2. They realize that the work of management is less a matter of "studentship" than of clear thinking, and a matter of commitment more than comparison (of how others practice it).

3. They realize that managers cannot operate from the love principle (no one likes to be pressed, yet the essence of managers' jobs is to bring about results that would not occur but for them).

Having those realizations causes managers to spend a minimum of time on gathering and interpreting information, checking to see how others have made decisions with which they are faced, and worrying about the impact on morale in making their decisions. The effective manager can be spotted because he spends most of his time in consideration of life-support information, ensuring that his decisions fit the circumstances of those particular decisions, and seeking to create high morale through achievement rather than through camouflaged appeals for affection.

Understanding and Mobility are Critical to High Productivity

Clarity of ideas and the hope of upward mobility are the two keys to obtaining full human contribution in business. Certainty of what must be done and recognition that doing it will produce rewards (increased right to individuality, involvement, authority, compensation, etc.) are essential to the establishment of goal-centered motivation.

Few companies take pains to ensure their organizations have both characteristics. True, a fair amount of effort is now being spent on the proceduralizing of communications and management, but both forms of effort tend to reflect poorly employees need to know of their true potential. Communication procedures are generally developed around each firm's business needs and manpower development usually is excessively constrained by top executive subjectivism and corporate tradition.

The foregoing would be of small consequence if the business wo.'ld were largely inhabited by self-motivated achievers. But the business world is inhabited mostly by persons who have little knowledge of what they or others want and who, if they are to be expected to progress in life at all, have to develop a confidence in that form of feedback they understand best: rewards given them for good performance.

Management Skill Is Not Technologically Based

The earlier given proposition - that the performance of almost every business can be improved by men determined to improve it - touches upon a number of vital considerations. Among them, the following have special relevance to our subject matter.

Perhaps the most powerful implication of the proposition is that management skill has a quite ordinary basis. The prime ingredients of effective management more are interest, common sense, and hard work than brilliance, way-out technology, or formal education. Any manager can improve his own and his company's performance by working harder at it with a more open and investigative mind. Techniques, such as financial modeling, and so forth, are useful, but not nearly as contributory as individual determination to do better.

Freedom Has Economic Value

Men do not produce at their best under constraint. They contribute most when they are free to be involved by their delights and sense of worth. That there is something of the truth in this view is attested to by current trends in management. A lot is heard today about decentralized management, participative management, and informal management. Studies indicate there is profit to be made in moving to "softer," less rigidly differentiated organization in which compartmental barriers between related positions are more permeable, men can operate with a minimum of control, and access to information is more democratic.

There is undoubtedly a good deal of factuality behind these indications. No doubt, responsibilities should be broadly felt with a minimum of hindrance from narrow assignments of duties, and personnel can benefit significantly from knowing as much about the company as they feel they need to know. But this must not be allowed to erode the conditions leading to high productivity. There is a world of difference between responsibilities being well-defined and being well-perceived.

Conformity Is A Business Requirement

The notion that the successful enterprise is one in which desired end results are achieved by a relaxing of discipline, which often accompanies moves toward more democratic, freer management, is not supported by one whit of evidence. It is probably closer to the truth to say that an organization successfully following a philosophy of decentralization and participative management has first done a top-notch job of working out its directional signals, setting standards for performance, and energizing its controls.

The idea that free enterprise is the cheapest, most efficient way to supply felt needs is viable only so long as it does not sweep into acceptance the ideas of laissez-faire and elitism. Freedom in business, as elsewhere in our world, can only be created within an environment of common understanding, motivation and commitment. Men cannot be free to contribute to their maximum and be rewarded according to their contribution in a gratuitous environment. Thus, we are faced with the seemingly anomalous condition that enterprise can only become as free as control over business affairs permits it. The proof of the pudding is contained in the fact that the successful enterprises in our business community are all characterized by well-established principles of operation, business philosophy and discipline. DuPont, IBM, Sears Roebuck and, more recently, Ford Motor Company and Control Data Corporation are good examples.

Thus, we must have conformity. As long as it does not descend to conformism, nothing is lost.

Authority Is A Resource

Every manager, sooner or later, faces the question, "What is authority?" In answering this, a further question is raised, "How shall I use it?" Taken together, the answers he gives to these two questions greatly affect his way of doing things. In turn, they control the success he is likely to achieve in doing his work.

Probably there is no word in the manager's vocabulary that is more misunderstood than authority. And none that carries with it more emotion-rousing connotations. That's not hard to understand because authority is usually linked in most minds with disagreeable ideas - with such words as command, order, coercion, force. Yet, almost to a man, we are convinced that, however much we may dislike it, authority is indispensable to achieving organizational success.

One of the toughest problems for all managers to handle is that of learning how to use authority properly. Without authority it's pretty hard to get things done; yet it's very use is dangerous to the purpose for which it is used. Failure to take people's feelings into account can seriously injure group objectives. On the other hand, authority which is too concerned with feelings may also result in a failure. We've also seen that authority doesn't work well without a system of rewards and punishment. Yet, authority which emphasizes such a system fails to enlist the best efforts of people.

In looking at the subject of authority, a number of characteristics are immediately apparent. Authority:

- always involves at least two people, the person who uses it, and the person who accepts it;

- is used to bring about desired actions;
- in and by itself, does not always succeed in achiev-
    ing its objectives.

If these characteristics are measured against the common view of authority - that is, originates with ownership, a board of directors, or the president of an enterprise, and flows downward - some real problems result.

The common view takes it for granted that the authority is in itself sufficient assurance that orders will be obeyed. Yet authority breaks down quite often. Therefore, either the common view of authority is wrong or our statement of characteristics is wrong. To choose the latter alternative is to ignore reality. So, it may be well for us to scrap the common view and start over again to try to redefine authority.

To begin with, a separation must be made between formal authority and accepted authority. We've seen too many examples of people exercising formal authority - and whose orders are consistently disregarded - for us to be fooled into thinking there isn't a difference. Furthermore, we've seen too many cases of managers who have given up their authority - because they don't know how to get orders obeyed - for us to accept the view that formal authority is a sufficient basis for getting orders accepted. Obviously, something besides authority - from-the-top, formal, or legal - is needed to get the job done. That "something" is acceptance of authority by the people to whom it is directed. To put it even more strongly, <u>authority can't produce results unless it is accepted by those who are subject to it.</u>

A radical statement? Not in our democratic society, it isn't! In a totalitarian system, "formal" and "real" authority are fairly close to the same thing. But, where a man has the free choice of working in order to reach his personal objectives, the acceptance of authority rests in those objectives and not in a charter of incorporation, by-laws or the chief executive of the organization. Hence, the acceptance of and the source of authority rests within the person subject to it.

Information Is What Resolves Uncertainty

Claude E. Shannon, a founder of information theory was the first to express this idea, so far as the author knows. Taken from information theory (the quantitative science of information) and applied to business, it is a brilliant idea with rich application to business problems.

If information can realistically be described as that which resolves uncertainty, then two things reasonably follow: (1) that which does not resolve uncertainty is not information (it is "noise") and (2) business information should be designed on the basis of the uncertainties of the business. If these are valid points it then becomes apparent that much of what passes for information in business does not qualify as information and, that few firms know much about the uncertainties that particularly affect them.

On the last score, two kinds of uncertainties face each business - those it shares with all other business enterprises and those peculiar to itself. Examples of the first lie in the forces at work in the economy in which the firm operates and which affect all firms in the economy. Examples of the second are those unique to each company, as determined by the content of knowledge, experience, and sensibilities resident in the total staff. Each firm must concern itself with both and take steps to be sure it is informed about changes with respect to both. But the second class of uncertainties is one that should receive special attention. Any business can be damaged by failing to keep the equivalent of an "iceberg watch" in the open seas, but it should never forget that far more ships have been sunk by failing to keep a sharp eye out for internal threats than by colliding with exterior objects.

Possession Of Information Bestows Power

As realization of the pertinence of system concepts to business grows, understanding of the importance of information also grows. What does not keep pace is the understanding that information itself can be a barrier to effective communication. The reason is simple: <u>information bestows power on its possessor</u>. For this reason, information tends to flow in direct proportion to its <u>unimportance</u>. People tend to hang on to information that has importance of one kind or another and pass along information that has little value.

This being the case, the trick in getting information to flow readily is to take importance of certain kinds away from information, such as novelty and rarity. Thus, an effective way to improve the flow of information is to introduce "information de-mocracy;" that is, make as much as possible of the information in a firm available to whomever desires it. Though this statement will seem to come to verge on the sacrilegious, it is a fact of commercial life that most information eventually becomes public knowledge regardless of the amount of security wrapped around it. Furthermore, most closely held information isn't worth being closely held. For example, executive salaries - one of the tra-ditional secrets of the typical firm - gain nothing by not being communicated and lose at least motivational value by not being openly known. Executive salaries hidden from view convey the impression of being undeserved rather than earned.

Managers Must Develop Themselves

As previously noted, effective managers have stand-alone capacity. They also have synthesizing minds.

These two qualities, vital though they are to sound decision-making, cannot develop in a manager through interaction with externals alone. No manager can accumulate enough experience or acquire enough information to be able to handle well every situation that will confront him, even though a day does not go by in which he is not forced to make decisions concerning situa-tions alien to both his experience and education.

Therefore, to be effective, a manager must also be in the grip of transcendant ideas - ideas that arise, perhaps, under the stimulus of observation but are more the products of reasoning and innovative thinking than perception.

Such ideas cannot be created to order and cannot, there-fore, be created through organized training and development ef-fort. No school exists where they can easily or necessarily be gotten. They are ideas that must rest well with the mind and such ideas can arise only from within. If that is true, then each person intending to be managerially competent must assume the responsibility for building his own managerial base. In short, topflight managers are not born or built; they are self-created.

That must eventually occur to anyone observing managerial performance or manager development for any length of time. No correlations have been established between formal manage-ment training or education and performance so far as the author

85

knows. If, then, an executive must be a generalist, as it is so often trumpeted in the so-called "management development" course and seminar field, what facility exists that can make him so except an internally provided gestalt?

Management Should Not Repress Conflict

Many managers regard their jobs as having a great deal to do with achieving and "maintaining the peace." Most managers would benefit their firms by doing more to stimulate differences.

This is not to say the managerial role should be exacerbating. But it is difficult to see how a progressive company can be also a quiet one. Persons operating at upper levels of their capabilities are certainly not going to be of one mind nor can a company benefit by having employees of one mode of sensitivity or motivation. A productive environment necessarily is going to feature the noise of contending points of view and expenditures of energy.

As long as that contention is not allowed to continue without being resolved by firm commitments and is not a result of deficient management, nothing will be lost and much can be gained by it.

Wilfulness Is The Prime Barrier To Exceptional Corporate Performance

This proposition has more to it than meets most eyes. The failure to perform well in business is usually attributed to shortages of capital, adverse market conditions, defective planning, and similar deficiencies. It must be admitted that these are among the ultimate reasons than they are supposed. In that class, there is probably no deficiency more heavily represented than that of executive willfulness.

Let's face it; business today is one of the richest sources of personal power and many executives have entered it to get power. Those who enter business for that reason cannot be expected to function in their firms' interests. They serve their own interests first, and the good they do is for the purpose of conserving the power they have achieved.

Of course, no man can be always objective. Even the best of managers will occasionally damage their firm's prospects by making self-serving decisions. But the best of managers do not make such decisions very often.

Business Success Founded On The Unusual

Decision-making that is knowledge-based and company-oriented is relatively rare. The garden variety of business decisions are safe, uninspired, conventional, and self-serving.

The "secret" of business success is to find and do the things that others do not think of or do not have the courage of doing. The steam engine, weaving machine, steel hull, automobile, electric generator, Xerox machine, and Wankel engine are the names of products that swiftly killed or may kill the markets for long established products.

If those statements are true, it then follows that determined men exercising common sense can really benefit their firms by making adventurous (unconventional), facts-based decisions. Executives cannot hope to significantly improve their firms' results until they start making decisions that are unusual in the firm's industry.

Justification for these views lies in two obvious facts:
1. Most businessmen's perspectives exhibit exceptional

uniformity (as to assumptions that bear critically upon decision making).

2. Outstanding corporate performance is rare (probably no more than 5 out of 100 firms are exceptionally well-managed). Taken together, these two facts strongly suggest the likelihood that outstanding corporate performance is closely connected with unusual management decisions or, and perhaps more accurately, decisions that implement unusual ideas.

Organize For Unknowns As Well As Knowns

Organization planners normally structure toward the operations and intentions of their firms - that is, toward the knowns or certainties of their corporate existence.

That is beyond criticism in and by itself. But it is not enough to ensure survival in the long run. Only when a company organizes toward its uncertainties as well as toward its certainties can the assurance be had that survival and high performance have reasonable chances of ensuing.

The foregoing language is a bit misleading. Nothing, of course, is certain except matters falling within the province of logic. In the real world certainty must be viewed as probability of the highest order - such as it is "certain that tomorrow will come." Similarly, every firm has, as it were, certainties that relate to it as a business institution and as a particular company. It is certain, for example, that if the firm fails to provide wanted products, it will sooner or later be forced out of business. Also, if it is in the fad toy field, say in hula hoops, it is certain that sooner or later the craze for hoops will pass away.

Now, as to the uncertainties, reflection will show that they are closely connected to its certainties. The firm in the fad toy field, for example, can be sure the high demand for hoops will slacken, but it cannot be sure when the turn-down will occur. Hence, the timing of that turn-down is one of that firm's uncertainties, and is one against which it must guard. One way it can guard is by setting up responsibilities for sales analysis that can give early warning when an established downward trend is detected.

APPENDICES

EXHIBIT I

"COGITO, ERGO SUM"
Merritt L. Kastens *

Skill in management, which is to say the talent for the effective direction of a complex enterprise, is seldom innate. There are just about the same percentage of natural-born managers in the human population as there are people with a natural golf swing. In other words, they do exist, but there certainly are not enough of them to conduct the multifarious affairs of our contemporary civilization. There may not be enough of them to support a good-sized golf club.

This fact has become apparent only in fairly recent times. A very few centuries ago a miniscule percentage of the population concerned themselves with the control and integration of other peoples' activities outside of their own family or clan. This small group was usually referred to as the "nobility." Even with the practice of the strictest genetic engineering, it proved impossible to breed a line of inherently skilled managers. The senior management, the would-be kinds, were traditionally trained in their craft from childhood. The director of management development was often known as the "privy counsel." The failures of their executive training programs account for much of what is in our history books.

The industrial revolution multiplied the employment opportunities for managers by at least an order of magnitude. There is little compelling evidence that the supply proved particularly elastic. The management techniques of the ascendent entrepreneurs depended primarily upon corporal punishment and economic repression. In this respect they borrowed heavily from their aristocratic predecessors.

From these brief observations, it might reasonably be inferred that the techniques of skillful management are not only not instinctive, but also in some respects unnatural. It would further

---

* "Cogito, Ergo Sum," INTERFACES, Vol. 2, No. 3, May 1972, pp. 29-32. Reprinted by permission of The Institute of Management Sciences.

follow that, being unnatural, they must be learned, and they must be learned at the expenditure of some considerable effort and no little discomfort. Most highly skilled athletes will testify that their most crucial movements seemed awkward and "unnatural" when they first experimented with them. The hit actress will usually confess that "naturalness" does not project a dramatic effect. The grand prix race driver does not survive for long if he depends on the reflexes adequate for ordinary road driving. "Common sense" is an explanation of, but not an acceptable excuse for, most of the bad management in the world today.

It is the discomfort, arising from the unfamilarity, the "unnaturalness" of the management process, which must account for the resistance of managers to the acceptance of more effective management techniques and for the prevailing low level of management practice in enterprises of all sizes and kinds. It is not that good management is so complicated or so difficult to comprehend. It is not that it requires an unusually high level of intelligence. It does not particularly require exotic skills in mathematics or computer science or applied psychology.

The problem essentially is that good management is uncomfortable. Until it becomes habitual, it requires the reversal of ingrained patterns of thinking. It means developing some new sets of mental muscles, and those muscles ache from unaccustomed use until they are conditioned to carrying a substantial load. It requires a powerful act of will to overcome instinctive assumptions about rewards and punishments. It requires the expenditure of a good deal of at least figurative blood, intellectual sweat, and possibly literal tears. It does not require magic.

The disconcerting intricacies of the management sciences with their arcane mathematical formulations and exotic symbolism do not bear directly on the management process. They deal primarily with analytical techniques for generating more precise inputs into the management process. The value and power of these techniques are in no way belittled by suggesting that they are not a substitute for management.

In a similar sense, the observations of the behavioral sciences regarding organizational behavior, group dynamics, motivation, learning processes have distinct bearing on management, but they do not in themselves define the management function.

"Getting things done through people" is not an adequate

definition of management either. It is in fact the most dangerous kind of malarkey. If this "buzz phrase" has any meaning at all, it applies with equal accuracy to demagoguery, spiritual inspiration, despotism, criminal fraud, hypnotism, as much as it does to management. As the phrase is most commonly interpreted in management literature, it is most nearly a definition of bureaucracy.

The pernicious danger of the management which this cliche reflects is that it is entirely directed towards "activity." The definition is critically mute on the subject of what "things" are to be gotten done. The result is mountains of unread job descriptions which delineate areas and quotas of activity, organization charts that define who is going to interact with whom but tell you nothing about what will be the subject of their interaction, salary reviews and bonus deliberations which have no way of relating to the contribution of the subject employee to the performance of the enterprise, and management-by-objective systems conceived as an instrument of individual development without reference to significance of contribution. A concept of management that focuses primarily on activity results in the proliferation of committee meetings, the pyramiding of levels of management, the 16-hour work day for executives, and an institutionalized mechanism for passing the buck.

The critical fact is that in no enterprise worth worrying about is there much likelihood of any person achieving a position of significant responsibility - that is, becoming a manager - who is not given to a high level of activity. The activity may have been motivated primarily by self-interest; it may have been phony scurrying about to impress the boss; it may have been a chaotic reflection of a basic confusion; it may have represented excess effort necessitated by fundamental incompetence. Hopefully it was a well conceived, highly productive effort reflecting a comprehensive appreciation of the problems at hand. One thing is certain; the guy has been moving around. Quiescent characters do not become managers. Therefore, we do not need a management system to guarantee that managers do things. Managers will do things by reflex, no matter how silly they are.

Unfortunately, although we are pretty safe in assuming that people who do not do things do not become managers, we have no like assurance regarding experience in thinking. It is quite possible to become a vice-president without ever having had a coherent thought in your life. We are not talking about ignorance or about intelligence. We are talking about the developed skill of considering complex matters within a comprehensive structure to derive a rational conclusion. Man may be a "thinking animal," but a thinking animal is not adequate as a manager if he thinks as an animal would think, in terms simply of what he is going to do next. To become a "rational animal," which is to comprehend the relationships of phenomena and the implications of actions over time, takes some practice.

Most management talent must be cultivated - it is not a volunteer crop. But the fruit of this husbandry must be rational capability to deal with complex patterns of cause and effect, not the rank foliage of pointless activity. The manager must have an increasingly sophisticated arsenal of procedural skills in order to practice management effectively, but the exercise of these skills does not in itself constitute management. The quintessence of management involves conceptual, abstract thinking, and therein lies the rub. Because the typical manager is naturally operation-oriented, he is uncomfortable dealing with generalized relationships. He tries to avoid the issue by hiring staff types, who are by temperament more analytical, to do his conceptualizing for him. He retreats behind such reassuring slogans as "experience," "hunch," "business savvy," "entrepreneurship," "leadership," or if he is somewhat more well read, perhaps "motivation" or "communication." He contends that his particular business environment is so unpredictable that rational actions are meaningless. He resists with considerable energy and some subtlety the necessity to endure the sore mental muscles that would be the price of actually thinking through the necessities and the possibilities of his position. And so he continues to act his way into blind alleys, sustains crises that could have been foreseen and prevented, sees his naive hopes of growth and profit blighted, and complains about the awesome demands of managerial responsibility.

Until managers and their mentors acknowledge that the ultimate essense of management effectiveness lies in rational thought processes, improvements in the general level of management effectiveness will continue to proceed at a glacial pace. New management techniques will be accepted slowly and implemented poorly because their value will not be apparent and in fact may be unrealized in many organizational environments. Managerial gimmicks, charts, and grids will continue to enjoy phenomenal vogues and then disappear. New names for long-recognized concepts will continue to be hailed as panaceas. The semantic fog created by the controversy over management as "art" or "science" will not dissipate.

Both art and science embody a large body of hard-won technique, but the techniques do not constitute either art or science. It is the philosophy of science which gives it its sometimes fearful power. Art which does not have its own inherent rationale does not survive.

It is the rationale of management that must be elaborated and propagated if management development is to have substantial impact! It is the quality of the thinking behind the actions that determines the quality of management. It is the resistance to new thought processes that so often thwarts the successful exploitation of even the most well-conceived new management techniques. Management must have an internal logic if it is going to justify itself at all. Certainly it must invoke an inherent causality if it has any pretenses to be a profession. It is in the understanding of the dynamics of that causality that management most often falls short. Enterprises stumble and sometimes fail not so much because managers are doing things wrong but because they are doing the wrong things. The logic of the relationship between decision-making and output-effect has been lost.

The academic disputes between the "humanistic" and the "mechanistic" schools of management theory are essentially sterile because they both focus primarily on the arrangement of activities within an organization. They tend to move rather casually over the fundamental fact that any organization exists - or should be permitted to exist - only in order to produce an incremental social or economic value. The effectiveness with which that end is achieved through the skillful application of accessible resources must be the final measure of management performance. But this criterion demands a high facility in relating causes and effects, which is a rational process. There is no way to master it except to think.

Cogito, ergo administro

EXHIBIT II

CHARACTERISTICS OF PLANNING

Before it is possible to talk sensibly about how planning should be done it is necessary to determine what the nature of planning is. If it is known what the elements of planning are, wherever and however performed, it becomes possible to move safely toward formal planning, despite limitations in planning experience.

The following facts about planning offers guides as to how planning should work:

1. planning is a process; a future-shaping activity - which planning spectacularly is - can be no less continuously or steadily progressing than the future with which it deals.

2. planning is a whole process; planning as a totality, as an unbound consideration of corporate needs, alone, can meet the future-shaping needs of a firm since each plan serves a specific purpose and cannot, in any case, be comprehensive.

3. planning is a multiplex activity; to be excellently performed, it calls upon the widest variety and combination of skills, knowledge, disciplines, and facilities.

4. planning is a reflexive activity; the planning process moves toward its final expression, an approved plan, through a recycling process (that is, it is seen and dealt with by the same people a number of times before being finalized).

5. planning is an in-bound activity; the process entails a fundamental directional flow in that planning information should gravitate from the general economic environment toward the purposes of the enterprise and specific organizational units (a characteristic that has given rise to the current interest in macro/micro economics).

6. planning is an inner-directed activity; planning must, if it is to justify its costs, be company-centered (always serving the survival and profit needs of the company doing the planning).

7. planning is a collegial activity; planning at any level gains and gives benefits in proportion to the numbers of people that participate in the process (that is, good plans always express the best thinking of and are known and understood by the largest percentage of those whose work is affected by the plans).

EXHIBIT III

THE PARAMETERS OF EFFECTIVE PLANNING

An effective planning function - wherever it exists - must result in these accomplishments:

1. it does not interfere with getting the most out of current operations, assets, and opportunities (successful firms do not fail to keep up what they are currently involved in while working toward better results in the future).

2. it focuses on making decisions affecting the future use of present resources (things never stay the same and the necessity to change is best anticipated).

3. it examines on a deliberate, organized basis the firm's external environment for existing but unseen and emerging situations offering the possibilities of new sources of profit (some changes should arise out of the assumption of new rather than altered current operations).

4. it produces plans for which costs of implementation have been estimated and resources requisitioned (a plan with resources committed is little better than a wish).

5. it produces plans resulting in profits far exceeding the costs of the plans themselves (plans should be laid only when the benefits are recognizably greater than the risks entailed).

6. it embodies the contributions of the firm's key people without burdening them with the work of forming the resulting plans (high performance is possible only when the most contributory staff members are free enough of detail to find problems and opportunities in place of finding how best to solve or exploit them).

It will be known that these accomplishments (and, therefore, effective planning) are within reach when the firm has:

1. guides to the identification and selection of corporate strategies (overall goals, philosophy of management, corporate policies).

2. plans that collectively cover every major aspect of the company's business and future prospects (long-range or strategic plans).

3. objectives that are fully supported by detailed plans

assigning the resources, time, and priorities required (variously called fulfillment, tactical, mission, or operational plans).

4. made planning coordination, support, and control the leading responsibility of one key executive (translation of goals and objectives into do-able work can only be assured when a singular and powerful responsibility for accomplishing it has been created).

5. given responsibility for the implementation of each plan to one person who has full authority to utilize the resources placed at his command as he sees fit, within the limits of the plan, to achieve the results planned (a plan should, whenever possible, have one person who participates on the setting of the plan held accountable for execution).

6. coupled each plan with a specially designed control system capable of signalling significant variances from the results intended.

7. adjusted the information system to provide feedback by which progress toward planned results can be measured, controls can be activated (as shown necessary by the appraisals made), and inputs can be made to corporate decision activities.

8. established a plan auditing function for measuring implementation progress independent of plan formulators, executors, or evaluators (plan implementation should be watched and controlled as every other business operation).

9. set up an organizational facility for reviewing audited plan implementation progress and final results and altering plan content or signing off the plan content or signing off the plan as successfully completed or abandoned.

EXHIBIT IV

A FIRM'S PLANNING OPPORTUNITIES

What each company should seek to accomplish through its planning efforts depends a great deal upon what it does well and what it does poorly. A company's strengths and weaknesses to a considerable extent determine what its opportunities and prospects are. For this reason it is important that the strengths and weaknesses receive close and forthright scrutiny before organizing to exploit the opportunities.

In attempting to perform this service (without being sophisticated about it), a planning executive in one very large firm with whom the author worked concluded that the company's main strengths were:

1. A topnotch name; the company's reputation for service, integrity, and dependability is good.

2. An assured supply of funds; the company has the history, connections, and investment opportunities to ensure continued access to sources of borrowing.

3. Superior business-producing connections; the company has better-than-average contacts for the discovery of quality investment opportunities.

4. Competent manpower; by-and-large the company's personnel are intelligent, experienced, well-regarded, and company-oriented.

5. Capacity to cope with detail; the company in the financing end of its business, at least) has a good deal of skill in managing an enormous amount of detail.

6. Freedom from endangering encumbrances; though more often counted as a lack of handicap than a strength the relative freedom from debt must itself be counted as a strength (because freedom of endangering encumbrances allows a firm to more fully exercise its powers).

7. National scale of operations; the company has representation across the country, a distinct asset to any firm that intends to be a significant factor in any national market.

A firm's principal weaknesses appear to be:

1. A faltering sense of direction; the company has no announced goals specifically enough to make clear its opportunities, options, priorities, or intentions, thereby reducing the burden of administration and communication (by giving operating personnel a basis for making short-range decisions without having constantly seek guidance and check to be sure they are not running afoul of a privately-held goal).

2. Lack of feedback that enables the firm to properly appraise its own performance; the absence of specific, realistic, and firmly held objectives limits the company to knowing how it has done (instead of the vastly more useful knowledge of how it might have done or could have done).

3. The company does not use its top people effectively; because of the lack of actionable plans (and therefore, early warning capabilities) the firm's principals are heavily engaged in rescue-and-repair instead of future-shaping work, which engagement makes heavy use of their experience but little use of their gifts.

4. The firm is not getting the best out of its work force; human beings are infinitely capable but the company's present orientation does not call upon the full range of its employees' capacities nor enable it to attract and/or hold high-potential personnel.

5. Lack of corporate dynamism; long corporate experience tends to become weighed down with barnacles and the firm has become encrusted by habit, uninspiring expectations, and unearned job security.

6. Lack of control over costs; large firms tend to accumulate people, methods, and equipment excessive to its real needs and we are lacking the benefits of a program aimed at trimming corporate fat.

7. The company does not benefit from the knowledge of business affairs available to it; the firm audits client operations heavily but leaves much of what it learns behind (that is, it does not bring back, consolidate, and creatively employ the knowledge of business affairs available to it).

The following goals are recommended as those which, if pursued vigorously, will help the firm to capitalize on its strengths and overcome or offset its weaknesses. The goals the firm

can aim for and is likely to profit most from pursuing are:

1.   Greater influence on the company's future; the firm ha~
been operating for a long time on a reactive basis and it can
much more creative in shaping its future.

2.   Managerial excellence; in our society profit no~
more from being well-managed than from the possessi~
terial assets and we should give top priority to the
being the best managed company in our field.

3.   Improved utilization of our knowledg~
most important of any firm's resources are th
content of the minds of the firm's people - a~
cated effort to make the fullest use of the ~
cannot fail to improve our performanc~

4.   Higher quality investment ~
principal profit tool at present is m
virtuosity and intelligence of its
tions for the funds at its comr

5.   Expanded opportu~
history of each firm has ~
how well it helps peopl~
to close the gap betwe~

6.   Perform~
our command ca~
out a network ~
meaningful ~

7. ~

presen~
past
ad~

a~

A~
accomplis~
such goals n~
approach to the ~

EXHIBIT V

THE ROLE OF THE TOP EXECUTIVE

A principal misconception in business - even among the most reputable figures in the field - is that the chief task of a firm's top executives is planning. This cannot possibly be true when the scale and character of planning activities are considered. It is more realistic to say that the impact of key executives on their firm's planning should be significant but that the work involved in creating implemental plans far exceeds the top executive time available. Viewing their businesses as wholes, spotting their firm's needs, and synchronizing the efforts to fulfill them should be the main work of top executives. The best inputs they make to planning stems from that work.

Plan development has two major elements: "seed" ideas and idea manipulation. By the first is meant the introduction into the planning process of ideas sufficiently worthy as to "turn on" the planning process. By the second is meant the process by which ideas are sought, stimulated, received, tested, and (upon approval) translated into plans, programs, standards, directions, and controls. The provision of seed ideas - ideas that have reasonable probability of and/or can precipitate many other ideas in the process of becoming an approved plan - is the more difficult of the two. Though the planning process itself will often show at least the vague outlines of ideas needed to fill gaps in strategies and tactics, only the business-oriented, creative mentality is a reliable source of "seed" ideas.

The main source of seed ideas is the company's key people, both because they have the needed overview and relative freedom from fixed tasks. Two implications with respect to larger corporation's top executives follow this statement:

1. top executives must have enough uncommitted time that seed ideas can arise and be formalized for presentation to the planning group.

2. top people should not take part in the evaluation or processing of seed ideas.

The importance of seed ideas becomes critical when a company needs ideas capable of redirecting its energies and resources along more profitable lines. But, such ideas do not arise gratuitously; they derive mainly in minds thoroughly familiar with the realities as they affect a company. Creating the ideas is a big task, not at all the "flash-of-genius" - "moment-in-time" thing it is so often claimed to be. In fact, so time-consuming is the task of being creative at the topmost level that the detailing of plans should be someone else's job.

INDEX

Titles in the
BUSINESS ALMANAC SERIES

Additional copies or titles may be ordered from:
Department BAS, Oceana Publications, Inc.
Dobbs Ferry, New York 10522

What You Should Know About
1. BOOKS FOR BUSINESSMEN: A BIBLIOGRAPHY compiled by Kent Kamy
2. DIRECT MAIL by Henry Hoke
3. RETAIL MERCHANDISING by Paul Crown
4. CUSTOMER RELATIONS by Arthur W. Einstein & Arthur W. Einstein, Jr.
5. SMALL BUSINESS CREDIT AND FINANCE by Eugene H. Fram
6. SMALL BUSINESS MANAGEMENT by Donald Grunewald
7. OPERATING YOUR BUSINESS AS A CORPORATION by Harold L. Krainin
8. LABOR RELATIONS by Julius Spivack
9. BUSINESS WRITING by Robert Koch
10. REDUCING CREDIT LOSSES by John H. Burns & John E. Cook
11. SMALL BUSINESS MARKETING by Eugene Fram
12. PERSONNEL MANAGEMENT by Howard Falberg
13. PUBLIC RELATIONS by Edward Starr
14. RESEARCH TECHNIQUES IN RETAILING by Howard Eilenberg
15. DATA PROCESSING by John E. Cook
16. ADVERTISING COPYWRITING by Shirley F. Milton
17. ADVERTISING by Joel Amstell
18. SELLING AND SALESMANSHIP by Milton B. Burstein
19. ACQUISITIONS AND MERGERS by Milton B. Burstein
20. BUILDING YOUR MAILING LISTS by Paul Crown
21. FOUNDATIONS OF MANAGEMENT by Roy Lindberg
22. SCIENTIFIC DECISION-MAKING FOR SMALL BUSINESS by Robin Lim